Religion and National Integration in Africa

Religion and National Integration in Africa

Islam, Christianity, and Politics in the Sudan and Nigeria

Edited with an Introduction by

JOHN O. HUNWICK

Northwestern University Press

EVANSTON, ILLINOIS

BP
64
.S8
R45
1992

Northwestern University Press
Evanston, Illinois 60201-2807

Copyright © 1992 by Northwestern University Press
All rights reserved. Published 1992
Printed in the United States of America

Library of Congress Cataloging-in-Publication Data

Religion and national integration in Africa : Islam, Christianity, and
    politics in the Sudan and Nigeria / edited with an introduction by
    John O. Hunwick.
        p. cm. — (Series in Islam and society in Africa)
    Includes bibliographical references.
    ISBN 0-8101-1037-7 (alk. paper)
    1. Islam—Social aspects—Sudan. 2. Islam—Social aspects—
Nigeria. 3. Christianity—Social aspects—Sudan. 4. Christianity—
Social aspects—Nigeria. 5. Sudan—Politics and government—1956–
6. Nigeria—Politics and government—1960– 7. Islam—Relations—
Christianity. [1. Christianity and other religions—Islam.]
    I. Hunwick, John O. II. Series.
    BP64.S8R45 1992
    322'.1'09624—dc20   91-45253
                                                                    CIP

The paper used in this publication meets the minimum requirements of
American National Standard for Information Sciences—Permanence of Paper
for Printed Library Materials, ANSI Z39.48–1984.

After this book had gone to press we were saddened to learn of the death of Mohamed Omer Beshir in London in late January 1992. We therefore respectfully dedicate this volume to his memory.

Contents

vii

Participants

Invited Speakers

ABDULLAHI AN-NA'IM, Professor of Law, University of Khartoum; Fellow at the Woodrow Wilson International Center for Scholars, Washington, D.C. Currently (1990) Professor of Law, University of Saskatchewan, Saskatoon, Canada.

FRANCIS DENG, former Minister of State for Foreign Affairs, Government of the Sudan; former Sudanese Ambassador to the United States, the Scandinavian countries, and Canada; Visiting Scholar and subsequently Research Associate, the Woodrow Wilson International Center for Scholars; Distinguished Fellow, the Rockefeller Brothers Fund; Jennings Randolph Distinguished Fellow, U.S. Institute of Peace, Washington, D.C. Currently (1990) Senior Fellow, Foreign Policy Studies Program, the Brookings Institution, Washington, D.C.

IBRAHIM GAMBARI, former Minister of Foreign Affairs, Federal Government of Nigeria; Professor of Political Science, Ahmadu Bello University, Zaria, Nigeria; Visiting Professor of Political Science, School of Advanced International Studies, Johns Hopkins University, Washington, D.C. Currently (1990) Nigerian Permanent Representative to the United Nations.

DON OHADIKE, Senior Lecturer in History, University of Jos, Nigeria; Visiting Professor, Stanford University. Currently (1990) Associate Professor, Africana Studies and Research Center, Cornell University.

Participants

LAMIN SANNEH, Professor, Center for the Study of World Religions, Harvard University. Currently (1990) Professor of Missions and World Christianity, the Divinity School, Yale University.

Commentators

MOHAMED OMER BESHIR, Professorial Fellow, Institute of African Studies, University of Khartoum; Visiting Scholar, Program of African Studies, Northwestern University; Member, U.N. Commission on Human Rights. Currently (1990) Director, Ahliyya University, Omdurman, the Sudan.

IBRAHIM ABU-LUGHOD, Professor of Political Science, Northwestern University.

DAVID LAITIN, Professor of Political Science, University of Chicago.

JOHN HUNWICK, Professor of History and of the History and Literature of Religions, Northwestern University.

Other Discussants

ABRAHAM DEMOZ, Professor of Linguistics, Northwestern University.

ABBAS HAMDANI, Professor of History, University of Wisconsin at Milwaukee.

LEMUEL JOHNSON, Professor of English and Director of the Program of Black and African Studies, University of Michigan, Ann Arbor.

LANSINE KABA, Director, Black Studies Program, University of Illinois at Chicago.

Preface

This volume contains the papers presented at a one-day seminar held in May 1988 at Northwestern University under the auspices of its Program of African Studies, as well as a transcript of the invited commentaries on them and the ensuing general discussion. Our focus was on the Sudan and Nigeria because they illustrate most graphically the problems facing African countries trying to weld together peoples of diverse cultures and histories into nation-states in the late twentieth century, a time when, at both the individual and the societal levels, a primary identification as Muslim or Christian often seems to override other loyalties. The seminar explored both the problems raised by religious loyalties and the underlying tensions of class, ethnicity, and the sharing of meager national resources. A final paper posing philosophical problems in the relationship of religion to the state gives a broader perspective and reminds us that such problems are not new ones.

Two Sudanese and two Nigerian speakers—in each case a Muslim and a Christian—were invited to give papers. They were asked not only to offer a dispassionate analysis of the situation in their respective countries, but also—because of their inevitable sense of involvement—to deliberate on possible solutions to the dilemmas their countries face as a result of the polarization of public opinion around widely differing philosophies of government and law. Formal commentaries were then solicited from faculty at or visiting Northwestern University and the University of Chicago, and at the seminar these were followed by discussion among the invited participants and questions and comments from the audience.

Preface

In preparing these papers and the transcript of commentaries and discussions for publication, I have attempted to standardize spellings of proper names and technical terms as far as possible. I decided, for example, to use *Sharia* rather than the technically more correct *Shari'a* to simplify preparation of the text and because the word now appears in English dictionaries with that spelling. Tapes of the commentaries and discussions were transcribed by Richard McGrail, to whom thanks are due for a tedious task well done. I then lightly edited the typescripts to ensure that what may have been quite comprehensible in an oral presentation at a conference could also be read smoothly and without serious danger of misunderstanding. Papers are arranged in the order of their presentation with commentary and discussion following as they did in the seminar. All participants were given an opportunity to revise their papers prior to publication. The versions here published of the papers by Dr. Deng and Prof. Ohadike differ considerably in form from those they presented; yet because the substantive issues they address are similar to those they dealt with in their conference presentations, the commentary and discussion sections are not rendered irrelevant.

John O. Hunwick
Evanston
July 1991

Introduction   JOHN O. HUNWICK

More than three years have passed since the Seminar on Religion and National Integration in Africa convened at Northwestern University. While I must offer apologies to the participants for the delay in getting the proceedings published, I believe that the delay has some advantages. First, very little of what the speakers and discussants had to say has become dated. The problems they addressed are still with us and their analyses of issues are as relevant now as they were in 1988. Second, it is now possible to examine subsequent developments in the Sudan and Nigeria—the two countries on which we focused—and see to what extent the prognostications of our speakers and discussants have proved sound. This introduction to the proceedings of the seminar will, therefore, attempt to provide an update in regard to the Sudan and Nigeria, while leaving the contributions of participants in 1988 to speak for themselves.

The Sudan

The Sudan has witnessed a number of dramatic events in the past two years. In late 1988 and the first half of 1989 it looked as if there might be prospects for an end to the civil war. The Umma party's junior partner in government, the Democratic Unionist party, sponsored a peace initiative in November 1988; then, in February 1989, the army sent a memorandum to Prime Minister Sadiq al-Mahdi calling on him either to bring the war to an end or to give the army the means with which to fight it. When he proved unable or unwilling to do either, on 30 June the army moved and ousted his civilian government. Lt.-Gen. Omar Hassan Ahmed el Bashir took over the reins of government at the head of a

Revolutionary Command Council for National Salvation. In fact, several army factions had considered a similar move, and one had been actively preparing a coup for 22 June when its leaders were rounded up four days beforehand.

From the outset it has seemed doubtful to outside observers that this new regime would succeed in bringing either peace or prosperity to the Sudan. In mid-1989 the country was essentially bankrupt, with debts of some $12 billion and payment arrears of $4.4 billion. Meanwhile, the regular army continued to lose ground to the Sudan Peoples Liberation Army (SPLA). To end the civil war, which is the key to beginning an economic recovery, clearly requires a massive political will—and a military regime is less likely than a civilian one to think in terms of a negotiated solution. Abdullahi An-Na'im, who was in the Sudan for several weeks immediately following the coup, concluded in the post-script to his paper that "at best, [the new junta may] succeed in introducing an element of temporary relief in the security and supply of essential goods situations in the Sudan, but it will be unlikely to end the civil war and achieve a peaceful and lasting settlement of the southern problem."

His pessimism seems justified in the light of subsequent events. Despite military aid from two friendly Arab countries, Libya and Iraq, a military solution to the civil war seems further away than ever. There has been considerable opposition to the new government's policies both from elements in the army and from civilians. Several purges of the army have been undertaken, through forced retirement, arrest and imprisonment, and, most recently, the summary execution of twenty-eight officers accused of plotting a coup in late April 1990. Civilian protests since October 1989 have led to the arrest and detention without trial of hundreds of trade unionists, doctors, academics, artists, and lawyers as well as the dismissal of about one thousand public servants.[1] In September 1989, civilian forces opposed to the government of Lieutenant-General el Beshir, including former Umma party stalwarts, southern political groups, and professional and workers organizations, formed a front known as the National Democratic

Alliance that has set up offices in Cairo, London, and Washington. In 1990, a monthly newsletter called the *Sudan Democratic Gazette*, edited and published by Bona Malwal, began to appear from London.

Although the military junta at first strenuously denied that it had sympathies with the National Islamic Front (NIF), its subsequent actions indicate that, on the contrary, the coup was designed to promote that party's interests. Dr. Hassan al-Turabi, who was originally detained, became upon his release the only former civilian politician allowed to travel freely outside the Sudan. Apparently through his efforts the "Islamic Call" organization (al-Daʿwā al-Islāmiyya) relocated its headquarters from Cairo to Khartoum—a move that was officially welcomed by Gen. Zubeir Mohamed Salih, deputy chairman of the Revolutionary Command Council, at a meeting of the organization in Khartoum on 12 May.[2] A number of "nonaligned" government ministers have recently been replaced by others who are NIF members or sympathizers: Abdel Rahim Mahmoud Hamdi at Finance, Mohamed Khojali Saliheen at Information, and Abdullah Mohamed Ahmed at Education.[3] The heads of all Sudan's universities were replaced in late March 1990 as part of the regime's "higher education revolution,"[4] which will stress the arabization of higher education but which is likely also to be a vehicle for its "islamization."[5] Finally, one may note the formation of Islamic "militias"—apparently an attempt at a kind of praetorian guard—which, it has been suggested, may eventually take over senior army positions vacated by dismissed, imprisoned, or executed officers.[6]

These developments do not appear promising for national integration. The military government in Khartoum seems determined to promote the interests of the hard-line Islamists, whose goal is an Islamic state and the implementation of Sharia as the law of the land, while at the same time attempting to settle the "southern problem" by winning the civil war and imposing its will on the non-Muslim segment of the Sudanese population.[7] In so doing it is alienating Western governments (in particular, the

United States) and building stronger bridges with certain of the Arab countries. On 2 March 1990, a union was announced between the Sudan and Libya; even before that, there were reports of Libyan air power being used against SPLA strongholds in the south.[8] Meanwhile, Libya is anxious to gain backdoor access to Chad, where anti-Habré (and often pro-Gadhafi) rebels are operating from bases in Darfur.[9] Iraq, now actively seeking an enhanced role in Arab politics, is also a player in this game, as it is in certain other sub-Saharan African countries, notably Mauritania.[10] The policy of Saddam Hussein's Ba'th Socialist regime is to give unqualified support to manifestations of "Arabism"; this translates into support for the *bīḍān* (Arabs) against the *sūdān* (blacks) in Mauritania, and support for the perceived "Arabs" (the Muslim northerners) against the "non-Arabs" (the southerners) of the Sudan. Both Libya and Iraq, moreover, are trying to score against Egypt, which is seeking to reemerge, after its post–Camp David isolation, as leader of the Arab world, though still endeavoring to remain a "moderate" despite loss of face over the stalled Israeli-Palestinian dialogue. Iraq has the largest and best-trained war machine in the Arab world, recently tested in the long Iran-Iraq war—a conflict in which some ten thousand Sudanese troops are said to have fought on the Iraqi side. It also has chemical weapons, as has (probably) Libya. The prospects for peace in the Sudan do not look good. The chances for dialogue and an emphasis on a common Sudanese identity that goes beyond religious and cultural differences—of which several of our seminar speakers were eloquent advocates—seem even more remote.

Nigeria

Although there has been sporadic civilian violence in Nigeria in the past two years, it has been occasioned more by protest against the belt-tightening that followed implementation of the Structural Adjustment Program than by interfaith antagonism. The fall in world oil prices in the 1980s left Nigeria's economy in a precarious position, and soon a crippling external debt mounted. Attempts to create confidence among international creditors, coupled with International Monetary Fund (IMF) pressure, led to an effective devaluation of the naira against the dollar by some 700 percent and the removal of internal subsidies (notably on petroleum products), which in turn fueled inflation. Interfaith antagonism, rather, has tended to manifest itself in what may be called a war of words—in public speeches, open letters, and magazine and newspaper articles. Nevertheless, it is not difficult to read a hidden message of interfaith antagonism in the attempt to overthrow Gen. Ibrahim Babangida's military regime on 22 April 1990. Although the coup leader, Maj. Gideon Orkar, in his single broadcast concerning the event never mentioned the word *religion*, his attack on "those who think it is their birthright to dominate till eternity the political and economic privileges of this great country to the exclusion of Middle Belt and the South"¹¹ would certainly have been read in Nigeria as an attack on the "Muslim" north for dominating the "Christian" Middle Belt and south.¹² During the past two years the "religion issue" has, in fact, never been far from the surface of debate over Nigeria's future—in particular, its future after the return to civilian rule in 1992¹³—and has, at times, threatened to dominate all other issues.

In my commentary on the papers of Professors Gambari and Ohadike in 1988 I offered the view that "there are too many cross-cutting factors to get away with any kind of monolithic Christian versus Muslim factions as a means of political opposition [in Nigeria]." Similarly, Professor Laitin remarked that "religious differences so cross-cut the discontent that it would be very difficult to build up a massive organization of the discontent based on some religious symbols." Such views may now need to be reconsidered. In the past two years there has, in fact, been a growing measure of consolidation among groups on either side of the religious divide, an increasing polarity between Muslim Nigerians and Christian Nigerians, and a harsher tone to mutual accusations of seeking to "dominate" Nigeria.¹⁴ This closing of ranks may reflect the fact that the new political arrangements for Nigeria announced by President Babangida in 1989 include as a central feature the institution of a two-party system. Although one party is to bear a label including the word *democratic* and the other will include the word *republican*, such labels have no real meaning in Nigeria. There have been no parties of any significance based on clear-cut political ideologies in Nigeria since independence in 1960—no "left" and no "right" in federal politics. The good intentions of the constitution of the Second Republic notwithstanding, politics has continued to show a stubborn tendency to remain rooted in regional or "ethnic" loyalties. Even so, the multiplicity of parties has generally had the effect of forcing disparate groups into political alliances and hence diffusing either north-south or Muslim-Christian tensions.

This situation may be changing as Nigeria moves toward the return to civilian government in 1992. The fear now is that the two parties that eventually emerge will, despite whatever labels they are given and whatever ban is placed on parties based on religion, essentially be one of Muslims and one of Christians. The religious affiliation of each party leader may itself determine to which banner Nigerians of either religion will flock, except in the unlikely event of both being Muslims or both Christians—a situation that would no doubt produce its own tensions. Accusations by Nigerian Christians that the Babangida regime is preparing to turn Nigeria into an Islamic state (with himself at the head of it) are growing ever more frequent and shrill. Among other things General Babangida has been accused of dropping Christians from his government in favor of Muslims and of replacing senior public servants who are Christians with Muslims. An open letter to the head of state by Christians from the eleven "northern" states of Nigeria quotes with approval a statement by the Christian Association of Nigeria, Northern Zone, that "the Babangida administration is the principal agent for the islamization of Nigeria."[15] This charge, in turn, tends to be connected to the contentious and still unresolved issue of Nigeria's membership in the Organization of Islamic Conference, with Christians alleging that Nigeria's full membership is dependent on its having the appearance of being an Islamic state.

Introduction

Muslim writers and intellectuals have tended to play the numbers game in response, showing that whatever the Christian-Muslim balance in high office may now be, it only reflects the demographic balance of the country as a whole, balance that hitherto has favored the Christians disproportionately; indeed, the whole superstructure of public life, they claim, has reflected a "Christian" ethos. Needless to say, the numbers game is incapable of accurate demonstration, given the lack of acceptable census figures since independence. Furthermore, the very fact that Nigerians are framing the debate in terms of balancing public office between Muslims and Christians is bound to cause apprehension about the future and call to mind the tragic experiences of Lebanon and Northern Ireland. After the traumatic civil war of 1967–70, Nigerians are justifiably wary of taking any path that may lead them in that direction again. Yet the declaration by the leader of the abortive April coup that five states of the far north were to be "excised" from the federation until the "real and recognised Sultan [of Sokoto] Alhaji Maciddo"[16] would lead a delegation "to vouch that the feudalistic and aristocratic quest for domination and oppression will never again be practised in any part of the Nigerian State"[17] shows that, within the army at any rate, some men are ready to risk civil war in pursuit of their goals.

One might simply write off Maj. Gideon Orkar as a naive ranter, but the severity of the fighting in Lagos at the time of the coup shows that he must have had considerable support (though how much of his program his fellow soldiers knew about is not clear). Had he been even slightly more successful, a major conflagration could have erupted within the army, which might easily have sparked conflict among civilians.

As in the Sudan, so in Nigeria, power struggles conducted under military regimes in a political vacuum are expressed in terms of "religious" issues. At stake, however, is the right to retain (for oneself) or impose (upon others) ways of life, patterns of behavior, systems of law, and expressions of culture. An atmosphere of distrust of the perceived "other" who is boxed with a Muslim

or Christian label is pervasive; all issues are in danger of being reduced to a single issue: faith. A deep sense of Sudanese-ness or
Nigerian-ness, of which several seminar participants spoke both
eloquently and passionately, is in real danger of being eroded
under the harsh realities of the new politics being played out in
the two countries.

Notes

1 Lists of those detained were published in releases by Africa Watch on 8
and 22 January 1990.

2 Republic of Sudan Radio, 12 May 1990; reported in *Sudan Update*, 18
May 1990.

3 See *Africa Confidential*, 19 April 1990.

4 The new appointments were announced by Republic of Sudan Radio on
31 March 1990; reported in *Sudan Update*, 20 April 1990.

5 The agreements to unify Sudan with Libya (signed in Tripoli on 2
March 1990) contain clauses that promise the spreading of the Islamic *da'wa*
and Islamic values across the world and the dissemination of Arabic language
and culture and its use in education. See *Middle East International*, 16 March
1990; and *Sudan Update*, 30 March 1990.

6 "Tribal militias" (Popular Defense Forces), formed with government
encouragement under Sadiq al-Mahdi's regime and accorded official status
under General el Beshir, have been responsible for a number of massacres in
Bahr el Ghazal, the southern Blue Nile, and the Nuba Mountains, including
the notorious ed Da'ien (March 1987) and el Jebelein (December 1989) massacres; see news release of Africa Watch of 23 January 1990. The "Islamic militias," in contrast, are urban-based. Popular Committees with a watchdog-vigi-
lante function have been established in the Khartoum area, and there is now a
Popular Defense unit for the capital manned by NIF personnel. For this and a
summary of other recent developments, see the report of David Hirst in the
Guardian (London), 29 March 1990.

7 General el Beshir has also held open the option of allowing (or forcing?)
the south to secede, thus allowing creation of a purely "Arab" Islamic state in
the north.

8 *Africa International* (Paris), no. 224 (February 1990): 10.

9 See *Africa Confidential*, 6 January 1989, 1–2.

10 See *Africa Confidential*, 1 December 1989.

11 As reported in *Punch* (Lagos), 24 April 1988, 8.

12 That this is so is demonstrated by the fact that it was found necessary
officially to deny such an interpretation. A letter from the Nigerian ambassador to the United States in the *New York Times* of 2 June 1990 states
that "the insurrection by a few officers . . . did not reflect religious division
in Nigeria or a north-south split. It was a sectional madness similar to the
abortive 1976 coup of Lieut. Col. Bukars [*sic*] Dimka. Last month's coup

plotters were merely a band of irresponsible and greedy officers, known to have accepted large sums of money to start the rebellion." Such an explanation, of course, raises more questions than it answers.

13 A debate on the place of Sharia in the constitution for the Third Republic in Constituent Assembly meetings in November 1988 became so acrimonious that General Babangida had to step in and halt discussion of the issue. A series of articles on the Sharia issue is contained in the *African Guardian* (Lagos), 24 October 1988, 19–26. For a defense of Sharia and a plea for its implementation, see Abdulmalik Bappa Mahmud (Honourable Grand Khadi, Bauchi State), *A Brief History of Shari'ah in the Defunct Northern Nigeria* (Jos, Nigeria: Jos University Press, 1988).

14 See reports in *Africa Confidential,* 2 December 1988, 5–6; 9 June 1989, 4–5. The Christian Association of Nigeria is an umbrella organization for the many Christian denominations and sects. On the Muslim side the Supreme Council for Islamic Affairs does a similar job, although severe antagonism exists between pro- and anti-Sufi groups. The so-called Sokoto Accord, designed to reconcile partisans of both Izala ("Wahhābī") and Sufi tendencies, was reaffirmed on 18 January 1988 in the wake of the local government elections of December 1987, in which Izala members had been advised to vote for Christians rather than "Sufis," and "Sufis" had voted for Christian rather than Izala candidates. See Muhammad Sani Umar, "Sufism and Anti-Sufism in Nigeria" (M.A. thesis, Bayero University, Kano, 1988), 222n.99.

15 The open letter is reproduced in part in *African Concord,* 5 February 1990, 36–37. The same issue of that magazine has a multicontributed article entitled "Before Nigeria Burns," with a summary box that reads: "Christians allege the gradual Islamisation of Nigeria. Muslims deny the charges and claim that the structures of the Nigerian nation are built on a Christian foundation. Religion assumes the centre stage in a macabre dance and Nigeria is perched precariously on the edge of a precipice."

16 Alhaji Maciddo, the eldest son of the late Sultan Abubakar III and a staunch traditionalist, was proclaimed sultan by the Sokoto "kingmakers" a mere two days after his father's death. Shortly afterward the Sokoto state government annulled this decision and proclaimed its support for another son, Ibrahim Dasuki—a move that led to severe rioting. Because Dasuki, a former diplomat and successful businessman, is known to be close to General Babangida, the reversal was widely interpreted as interference in Sokoto's affairs by the Nigerian head of state. This situation, coupled with the recent elevation of another pro-Babangida member of the Sokoto "royal" family, Alhaji Abubakar Alhaji, to the office of Sardauna of Sokoto (vacant since Sir Ahmadu Bello's assassination in January 1966), has led to speculation that Babangida is trying to establish a power base in Sokoto, where he has hitherto been unpopular. In extreme versions, a conspiracy theory emerges that would see Babangida, having parted company with his (largely Christian) Middle Belt supporters (notably the "Langtang mafia"), seeking to ally himself with traditional power structures of the Islamic north to support his bid to remain as president after the return to civilian rule. See *Africa Confidential,* 6 April 1990, 3–4.

17 See *The Punch,* 24 April 1990, 8.

Islam and National Integration
in the Sudan   ABDULLAHI A. AN-NA'IM

Introduction

Strict adherence to a monotheistic religion such as Judaism, Christianity, or Islam has often been perceived as necessarily exclusive. The monotheistic creed itself usually perceives of God as being extremely jealous, demanding of believers total loyalty without association with any "other." It is not surprising, therefore, that whenever that conception of the monotheistic creed is made the effective basis of collective political identity it tends to exclude nonbelievers according to the degree of their nonbelief. Similarly, the ideal constitutional and legal system of such a monotheistic belief would treat its subjects according to their relationship with the underlying belief.

Yet despite the strenuous efforts of adherents and the horrendous suffering of perceived or real enemies and opponents, none of the monotheistic creeds has managed to maintain itself as the exclusive basis of collective political identity or to establish its constitutional and legal system over extensive territory for a significant period of time. The pure polity of believers has remained, throughout history, an unattainable ideal. Believers have always had to contend with the existence of unbelievers and cater to their demands and expectations as fellow human beings.

Faced with this reality, Christian Europeans took the lead in formally and explicitly abandoning the monotheistic ideal of a monolithic polity and modifying the role of religion in public life, thereby opening the way for the development of what is known as the secular nation-state. This shift was facilitated within

Christianity by the belief that Christ himself was unconcerned with temporal affairs. Yet because this interpretation of Christ's position took several centuries of struggle and suffering to evolve, it may be assumed that it was prompted by other intellectual and practical considerations. Moreover, it would appear that the modification of the role of religion in public life was a necessary but insufficient condition for the development of the modern nation-state. Costly wars and painful economic and political adjustments have had to be endured since; and more may be in store for the nations of Europe and those who followed their example.

For centuries after the European Christians took that significant step, the Muslim peoples of the world continued to hold fast to their ideal of the universal Islamic state. Unlike Christ, Muhammad was clearly very concerned with the temporal affairs of his followers and in fact established the concept of *umma*, of community and political unity among believers. Moreover, based on this ideal Muslim jurists have developed a systematic and comprehensive legal order, the Sharia, which the community and its rulers are supposed to implement in practice.[1] Thus, while their governments had little to do with the community envisaged by the Prophet, and their public affairs reflected little true conformity with Sharia, Muslim peoples have always maintained their faith in these ideals and hope for their realization.[2] So long as their rulers expressed commitment to implement Sharia, Muslim peoples were willing to wait for the fulfillment of the ideal.[3]

In the meantime, however, local and general circumstances have changed so much that they bear almost no resemblance to those prevailing at the time of the original conception of the Muslim *umma* in which the Sharia is supposed to be implemented. In particular, Muslim peoples have come to accept, and even insist on, the pluralistic nation-state as the basis of their domestic and international relations.[4]

Whereas in the West the nation-state and the international order that regulates relations among states have evolved gradually out of the experience of European peoples, these institutions were suddenly but effectively imposed on the Muslim peoples, especially during the colonial period. Now that the colonial period, at least in its original form, is over, Muslims find themselves facing a real dilemma. On the one hand, they are politically independent and free to pursue their Islamic ideal; on the other hand, the practical circumstances under which they must operate make it impossible to achieve that ideal in its historical conception. The realities of the nation-state and the international order on which it is predicated are irrevocable; yet they are also irreconcilable with the original notion of *umma* and the historical formulation of Sharia. Moreover, given the close link between the Islamic moral order and the political regime of the Muslim polity, an explicitly secular approach does not seem a viable option in the Muslim context.[5] Is it possible for modern Muslims to evolve a formula that would enable them to realize their Islamic ideal within the practical context of the present nation-state and international order?

I suggest that, although it is impossible to reconcile the original notion of *umma* and the historical formulation of Sharia with the modern nation-state and international order, the reverse may be possible. In other words, perhaps the Islamic ideal can be redefined by interpreting the fundamental sources of Islam, namely the Qur'an and Sunna, or Traditions of the Prophet, in a way that will provide modern Muslims with both a new sense of collective identity, one consistent with the realities of the multireligious nation-state, and the appropriate constitutional and legal order. Such a modern conception of an "Islamic" collective identity and public law would be conducive to national integration rather than detrimental to it.

This proposed Islamic reformation is similar to the Christian reformation in one respect and different from it in another. The two are similar in that the proposed Islamic reformation is now being prompted by certain contextual intellectual and practical developments in the same way that its Christian counter part was several centuries ago. They differ in that the Christian reformation relied on the perceived dissociation of religion and politics during the founding stage of Christianity itself, whereas the Muslim reformation cannot help but address and work with the commonly perceived association of religion and politics.

I will now develop these general remarks with specific reference to the Sudan. After a brief explanation of the concept of national integration, I will outline the process of islamization in the northern Sudan and highlight the generally moderate and tolerant nature of the northern Sudanese Muslim population. As we shall see, Sudanese Muslims have not in the past pursued the historical model of the Muslim *umma* under Sharia except perhaps briefly in the Mahdist state of the late nineteenth century. Nevertheless, upon independence from Anglo-Egyptian rule in 1956 an immediate call was raised for adoption of an Islamic constitution and application of Sharia. I will continue by explaining the positions of the main political forces in the country and the implications of those positions.

Although the May regime of former President Nimeiri began its rule in 1969 on the left of Sudanese politics and gravitated toward the center by the mid-1970s, it was this regime that imposed Sharia and attempted to establish an Islamic state by 1983. The background and impact of this legislative coup d'état will be discussed in the next section of the paper, followed by a review of the positions of the main political forces in the country in light of recent developments, after the overthrow of Nimeiri on 6 April 1985 and the country's return to its earlier state of constitutional transition and debate over the public role of Islam. I will close with a reflection on the experiences of over thirty years of independence and assess the prospects for a positive or negative impact of Islam on national integration in the Sudan. A "postscript" casts a glance at the situation in light of the coup d'état of June 1989.

Of National Integration

The term *national integration* as I use it raises questions about the nature of nationhood and the form and degree of integration contemplated in the Sudan. As Rupert Emerson correctly points out, there is much that we unjustifiably take for granted in relation to nationalism.[6] In fact, there is no real agreement as to what a nation is.[7] Despite this lack of consensus, it is sometimes assumed, "often implicitly, that each nation is a preordained entity which, like Sleeping Beauty, needs only the appropriate kiss to bring it to vibrant life—and perhaps even that it was willfully put to sleep by some evil genius."[8] This assumption is based partly on the fact that the first nations to make themselves evident in modern history, such as France, embraced peoples who had already achieved a large measure of internal unity. Yet even in the case of France, the further back the inquiry is pressed, the less inevitable it seems that this particular France should have emerged from the long course of history.[9] The same is even more true of almost all other modern "nations."

Moreover, while even the best-established nations were at some point a congeries of stocks and tribes, those peoples were welded together into nations before the general populace became aware of their rights and powers. In contrast, the modern African nationalist is confronted with the complex task of welding diverse peoples into a nation at a time when the masses are becoming increasingly aware of their political rights and powers, including the right and power to affect the scope and nature of the nation to be. Consequently, to establish a political entity that controls the territory designated as a "nation" does not necessarily mean that it is inhabited by people who conceive of themselves as such.

This sense of affinity, a feeling that one shares deeply significant elements of a common heritage and a common destiny, is what makes a nation.[10] Moreover, since generally one lives the destiny of one's nation, it is important to secure a coincidence of nation and state, thus enabling the nation to protect and assert itself and enabling its citizens, at least in theory, to control their destiny. Nationalism, then, has become the basis of legitimacy for the modern state.[11] The state is supposed to be the vehicle of the nation, the means of achieving its integrity and well-being.

Nevertheless, despite the preeminence of the nation-state, other forms of community are possible. Family, tribe or ethnicity, religion or conscience, economic interests, and many other senses of identity may claim people's allegiance. Whenever such "narrower" allegiance is seen as inconsistent with the "broader" allegiance to the nation, the latter is supposed to prevail, presumably through the supreme coercive power of the state. That power, however, itself depends on men and women in the mass acknowledging the legitimacy of the demands the nation-state makes upon them, and accepting the nation as the community that most nearly embraces all aspects of their lives.[12] No state is powerful enough to impose its will on its population without the willing cooperation of that population.

It would therefore seem desirable to minimize conflict between allegiance to the nation and other forms of allegiance. This brings into focus the question of the degree and form of integration that is necessary for peoples to become a nation. I suggest that while a degree of national integration is necessary, total integration is neither possible nor desirable. Human beings need and in fact experience numerous identities and will not abandon them in favor of a single, monolithic national identity. Any state, however powerful it may be, needs popular acceptance of the validity and reasonableness of its claims on the population at large; this will not be forthcoming if the state asks people to give up their ethnic, religious, or other essential bases of identity.

Coercive power, moreover, to the extent that it is possible to impose it on a minority of the population, is antithetical to the very notion of national integration. No people, whether identified by ethnicity, religion, or some similar factor, are likely to be successfully integrated into the body of a larger "nation" against their will. It will just be a matter of time before such a group finds a means of challenging forced national integration and of asserting a separate identity. Countless examples of this phenomenon can be cited from around the world today.

A balanced approach to the manner and degree of national integration must be maintained. Not only must the process be voluntary and gradual, but it must also concede the need of the population for other forms and levels of identity. For the process to be voluntary, all segments of the population must see that it is in their best interest to be part of the nation. This will occur only if people are not rushed into a single whole at the expense of other values they cherish and hold essential for their dignified existence.

Because it is not possible to address all aspects of the process of national integration in the Sudan, the rest of this paper will focus on the central theme of equality among all members of the nation-to-be. In particular, it will address the threat to legal equality of all Sudanese posed by the recent application of Islamic Sharia law. Obviously, legal equality does not necessarily lead to substantive equality among all groups and individuals; much more effort is needed to achieve all forms of economic, political, and social equality. Nevertheless, legal equality is essential to achieving other types of equality. In other words, legal equality is a necessary but insufficient condition for achieving broad equality.

I believe that this necessary but insufficient condition has been seriously challenged by the recent application of Sharia throughout the Sudan; I also believe, however, that the situation can be rectified. In fact, I find some of the recent developments rather surprising and not reflective of the thinking of the vast majority of the population. Given the history of religious attitudes and practices among northern Sudanese Muslims, it seems implausible that they would really wish to impose their will on the non-Muslim Sudanese, thereby threatening the process of national integration and repudiating the prospects for political stability and economic and social development.

The Islamization of Northern Sudan

Islam came to the northern Sudan through the gradual migration of Muslim tribes from Egypt and North Africa and their integration with the local Christian population of the Middle Nile Valley, rather than through military conquest. Following the establishment of an Islamic regime in Egypt in the second quarter of the seventh century, the Christian kingdoms of northern Sudan maintained their political independence for seven centuries until finally they were taken from within by an islamized local population.[13] As the nature and duration of the process of islamization indicate, Muslims and non-Muslims have coexisted peacefully in northern Sudan for centuries, under both Christian and then Muslim rule.

Moreover, there was an early and significant Sufi influence on the northern Sudanese. Muslim Sufi masters have generally accepted the authenticity of non-Muslim religious experience[14] and encouraged introspective reflection on the part of their followers, thus synthesizing local elements of the people's culture and "external" Islamic elements.[15] Hence, although several factors may have contributed to the atmosphere of mutual toleration in the islamized northern Sudan, the Sufi influence was especially significant in fostering a spirit of moderation and tolerance.

During the era of the Funj sultanate of the Nile Valley (1517–1821), the Dar Fur sultanate (ca. 1650–1916), and other Muslim kingdoms and polities of present-day western Sudan, Islam became the dominant religion. While this political consolidation introduced an element of Islamic officiality, in that the state structure began to reflect some Islamic features, strict Sharia was never applied systematically during that period.[16] The Turco-Egyptian administration of 1821–84 continued the same policy of limited enforcement of Sharia in private and personal law but not in public life, as was the trend in Egypt itself and throughout the Ottoman Empire at the time.[17] By and large, the local population was left to fend for itself through customary law and practices, which comprised both Islamic and non-Islamic components.

Yet the puritanical Muhammad Ahmad ibn Abdullahi saw these same elements of Sufi and official tolerance and moderation as adulteration of the faith. Announcing himself Mahdi, the divinely chosen and guided one, Muhammad Ahmad set out to purify the faith and rectify the believers through his religiopolitical revolution of 1881–84.[18] By January 1885 he had succeeded in capturing Khartoum and establishing the Mahdist state throughout most of present-day northern Sudan. Following his death six months later, his successor, the Khalifa Abdullahi, extended and consolidated Mahdist rule to most parts of southern Sudan.

Although the Mahdi, and the Khalifa Abdullahi after him, purported to apply strict Sharia in establishing a truly Islamic state, in practice it was the Mahdi's own version of Sharia and the Khalifa's political expediency that prevailed. Remaining true to their traditions of moderation and tolerance, many Sudanese Muslims found the Mahdist state oppressive and repugnant. This fact is evidenced by two main features of the period: continued domestic dissent leading to the execution and imprisonment of large numbers of Sudanese community and tribal leaders, and northern Sudanese collaboration in Anglo-Egyptian efforts to recapture the Sudan. When these latter efforts finally succeeded in 1898, the Sudan was placed under the Anglo-Egyptian Condominium administration.

This administration, having reconquered the Sudan on behalf of Egypt after the violent and temporarily successful Mahdist religious revolt, was at first worried about the role of Islam in Sudanese politics. Hence, Islam was rigorously excluded from playing a role in Sudanese public life. By the late 1920s, however, the British faction of the Condominium began to work with Abd al-Rahman, the son of the Mahdi, and his Ansar community, encouraging him to assume a modest political role in order to counterbalance the growing influence of Egypt in the country. For their part, the Egyptians adopted al-Sayyid Ali al-Mirghani and his Khatmiya order as their champions in the Sudan. Thus, despite initial suspicions about the role of Islam in Sudanese politics, both partners in the Condominium came to encourage such a role as a means of bolstering their respective positions in the country.

This colonial policy, I suggest, has had a long-term negative impact on national integration in the independent Sudan because it helped cast national politics in terms of religious allegiance to the two main Islamic groupings in the country, the Ansar and Khatmiya. By co-opting the intellectual leaders of the modern nationalist struggle for independence, the Islamic religious leaders of these two sects have succeeded, in my view, in committing the national parties to a narrow Islamic platform. The Condominium administration also retarded national integration through its "closed district policy," which, by denying Sudanese freedom of movement between northern and southern Sudan, deepened the rift between the two parts of the country and retarded natural cultural and racial integration.

The Debate over the Role of Religion Since Independence

Owing to the politically active nature of Islam and its predominance in the country as a whole, the debate over the role of religion in public life since independence has always focused on Islam. To understand this debate and its implications for national integration, we need to recall a few facts about the public-law aspects of Sharia, because it is how these aspects are applied that is supported by some and opposed by others. (Private-law aspects of Sharia, such as family law and inheritance, have always affected only Muslims and are, generally speaking, of no concern to non-Muslims.) The status and rights of non-Muslims under Sharia, however, have peculiarly important implications for national integration.

Sharia and Non-Muslims

Sharia, as a comprehensive and systematic legal system, was developed by the founding Muslim jurists of the eighth and ninth centuries; yet it is derived from the Qur'an—believed by Muslims to be the literal and final word of God as revealed to the Prophet between 610 and 632—and the Sunna of the Prophet.[19] Although parts of the Qur'an were recorded during the lifetime of the Prophet, the complete text (al-Mushaf) was collected and officially promulgated during the reign of Uthman, the third caliph. Sunna, however, remained an oral tradition for nearly two centuries until it was collected and recorded by specialized jurists in the eighth and ninth centuries. Whereas little, if any, significant disagreement prevails among modern Muslims over the text of the Qur'an, strong controversy continues over the authenticity of many texts of Sunna and their relationship to the Qur'an.[20]

Because of these controversies over Sunna and differences over the interpretation of the Qur'an, Muslim jurists disagree on almost every general principle or detailed rule of Sharia.[21] For almost every position held by an individual jurist or school of jurisprudence, one can find a different, if not the opposite, position held by another jurist or school of jurisprudence. Such a wide diversity of opinion may have been both unavoidable and even useful for the flexibility and adaptability of Sharia to different localities and changing circumstances in the past, but it raises serious problems for the modern applicability of Sharia. Whereas previous conditions of transportation and communication permitted the application of different, context-specific opinions on the rule of Sharia, modern conditions require greater certainty and predictability in the law for domestic and international purposes.

Here, let us focus on those aspects of Sharia that enjoy the widest acceptance by the most authoritative and best established jurists and schools of jurisprudence. It must be emphasized, however, that we are concerned with the relevant principles and rules of Sharia as historically determined by the founding jurists and accepted by the majority of Muslims. I fully concede the possibility of an alternative interpretation of the Qur'an and Sunna on public-law issues; in fact, I will later propose such an alternative interpretation for the issues raised in the following discussion. First, though, we must identify the relevant principles and rules of Sharia as they already exist. In other words, we have to be clear on what Sharia *is* before we can discuss what it ought to or can be.

Constitutional Status and Civil Rights. Regarding the structure of an Islamic state under Sharia and its provisions for both Muslim and non-Muslim subjects, the most authoritative model remains the one established by the Prophet in Medina after his migration from Mecca in 622.

In fact, though, the model Sharia state of Medina did *not* provide for many of the constitutional mechanisms and limitations of power that we take for granted today.[22] For example, selection of the ruler can hardly be described as popular election in the modern sense of the term.[23] Moreover, the extent of the ruler's powers and the mechanisms for holding him to such limitations as existed under Sharia are clearly unsatisfactory by modern constitutional standards.[24] Nevertheless, let us for the sake of argument assume that such problems can be resolved through imaginative reading of the earlier formulations of the relevant principles of Sharia and instead focus on the most definite and problematic aspects of Sharia as they apply to national integration in a multireligious modern nation-state.

Under Sharia, the subjects of an Islamic state are strictly classified in terms of religion or belief. At the top of the hierarchy are Muslims who enjoy full legal status under Sharia; they have complete access to any public office in the state.

The next class comprises the *ahl al-kitāb*, those who believe in God in accordance with a divinely revealed scripture (primarily Jews and Christians). This group may be offered a compact of *dhimma* with the Muslim state under Sharia, which guarantees security of their persons and property and freedom to practice their religion, as well as some freedom to apply their own law in personal matters.[25] In return, *dhimmīs* must submit to Muslim sovereignty and pay *jizya*, a poll tax, to the Muslim state as a token of that submission. As subjects rather than citizens of the state, *dhimmīs* have no right to participate in the government of the state as a whole, although they enjoy a degree of autonomy in their communal affairs.[26] Moreover, *dhimmīs* are subject to other disqualifications under Sharia, some of which will be indicated below. While other non-Muslims were not originally entitled to receive *dhimma* status under Sharia, they might be permitted to enter and remain in the territory of the Muslim state through special *amān* (safe conduct). If they were allowed to stay for more than one year, they may be treated as *dhimmīs*, and as such be entitled to the benefits and subject to the limitations of that status.[27]

Criminal Justice. Criminal offenses under Sharia are divided into three classes: *ḥudūd, qiṣāṣ*, and *ta'zīr*.[28] According to the majority view, *ḥudūd* (sing. *ḥadd*) are those offenses for which strict punishments are specified by either the Qur'an or Sunna: *sariqa*, theft; *qaṭ' al-ṭarīq*, highway robbery; *zinā*, fornication; *qadhf*, unproven accusation of *zinā*; and *shurb al-khamr*, drinking wine.

Some jurists would add two more *ḥudūd*: *ridda*, apostasy by a Muslim; and *baghy*, rebellion. In all *ḥudūd*, neither the victim nor the authorities have any choice but to inflict the specified punishment once the offense is proven.

Qiṣāṣ covers homicide and other forms of bodily injury, acts punishable either by direct retaliation on the culprit or by payment of *diya*, monetary compensation. Although this penal principle is provided for in the Qur'an itself (for example, verses 2:178 and 5:45), these offenses are not *ḥudūd* because the Qur'an allows the victim or his or her surviving kin to enjoy complete discretion in choosing whether to forgive the culprit altogether, to exact retaliation, or to accept compensation.

Ta'zīr is in fact the discretionary power of the ruler or his representative to punish any type of conduct other than a *ḥadd* or *qiṣāṣ* offense. In an attempt to restrict the excessively vague and arbitrary nature of this power, some jurists have suggested guidelines as to just what acts may be punished under the power of *ta'zīr*.[29] Nevertheless, as a matter of Sharia, the ruler has very broad discretion in deciding both what conduct to penalize and what punishment to impose.[30]

According to Sharia, this scheme of penal measures applies throughout the territory of the Islamic state and is binding on all its subjects, Muslims and non-Muslims alike, unless Sharia itself makes an exception for non-Muslims. (The only general exception in favor of non-Muslim subjects is that they may drink alcohol, a *ḥadd* offense for Muslims.)

The enforcement of this penal law consequent on the establishment of an Islamic state is thus problematic as regards non-Muslim subjects. For one thing, Sharia punishments for *ḥudūd* are as a rule extremely harsh. The required punishment for theft, for example, is amputation of the right hand; that for highway robbery, cross-amputation of the right hand and left foot. While an unmarried person convicted of fornication is punishable by one hundred lashes, a married person is to be stoned to death. Muslims may accept such harsh punishments not only because their religion clearly specifies penalties for specific acts, but also because enduring such punishment in this life is believed to absolve the culprit in the next life. Neither of these grounds is applicable to non-Muslims.

Other aspects of the penal law of Sharia would be unacceptable to non-Muslims as well. For example, most jurists would not allow the Muslim murderer of a non-Muslim to be executed. Moreover, if the surviving kin wanted to accept monetary compensation for an offense, *diya* for a non-Muslim is much less than for a Muslim.[31] Non-Muslims would also find Sharia rules of evidence objectionable, in that a non-Muslim is not considered a competent witness against a Muslim facing a *ḥadd* and *qiṣāṣ* charge, whereas the reverse is not the case.[32]

The Nature and Terms of the Debate in the Sudan

Given these and other aspects of Sharia, it is incredible that any responsible leader would advocate its application in a modern multireligious nation-state like the Sudan. Yet this has been the declared position of the major northern political parties, subject to the following qualifications.

Although the Umma and Unionist parties (with the Ansar and Khatmiya as their respective political constituencies) have expressed their commitment to the full implementation of Sharia, there is good reason to believe that their leadership is ambivalent on this fundamental issue. For one thing, whereas these two parties have ruled the Sudan, in a variety of coalition combinations, during all the nation's "democratic" phases—1956–58, 1964–69, and 1986–89—their record in implementing an "Islamic" constitution and applying Sharia has never lived up to their declared intentions. Then too, these two parties were the main political force behind the three transitional constitutions of 1956, 1964, and 1985, all of which have guaranteed equality before the law and freedom from discrimination on grounds of religion—provisions clearly inconsistent with the above-noted aspects of Sharia. Significantly, though, both parties also supported the draft constitutions of 1958 and 1968, which reflected a strong commitment to implementing Sharia.

Thus, it is difficult to assess the commitment of the two main parties to the implementation of a Sharia state. In fact, it is debatable whether the leadership of these parties is really familiar with the constitutional implications of their declared positions. In any case, instead of a clear statement of the exact Sharia model they envisage, these leaders make contradictory statements on the subject. For example, they declare their commitment to apply Sharia while *fully safeguarding the citizenship rights of non-Muslim Sudanese.* Since Sharia does not recognize full rights of citizenship for non-Muslims, one part of that statement will have to give way to the other. It should be emphasized that so long as judicial, executive, and administrative organs interpret and apply Sharia as it was established by Muslim jurists in the past, there cannot be equality between Muslim and non-Muslim Sudanese. In other words, unless party leaders follow their pledge to achieve equality with the enactment of specific laws that guarantee such equality in practice, their promise will remain an illusion.

Whereas the leadership of the Umma and Unionist parties may be seen as having been forced into their positions by Islamic political constituencies, the National Islamic Front (NIF) has actively created such a constituency for itself. A commitment to implement Sharia has always been the primary goal of the Muslim Brothers, the NIF hard core, and it is the clear message of all public documents issued by the front. Even so, an element of ambiguity marks the position of the National Islamic Front. While openly committed to the implementation of Sharia, the front continues to misrepresent Sharia in order to minimize its negative impact on non-Muslim Sudanese.[33]

Both the ambivalence of the Umma and Unionist parties and the ambiguity of the National Islamic Front can be understood in light of the existence of a politically strong and militant non-Muslim minority in the Sudan, which has always opposed the imposition of Sharia on non-Muslim Sudanese—even though members of this non-Muslim minority do not appear to be fully aware of the extent of their loss under Sharia.[34] For the most part, I believe, the opposition of non-Muslim Sudanese is in an emotional and psychological reaction against domination by the north. If their leaders had educated themselves in Sharia, they would have been able to make a more coherent and rational case against the application of Sharia in a country like the Sudan.

Other minor political parties and forces in the north are opposed to the implementation of Sharia as well, including the Sudanese Communist party and professional and trade unions, whose leaders favor a secular state. Although as educated Muslims these northern Sudanese may be knowledgeable about the problems that accompany the modern application of Sharia, they find it difficult to criticize Sharia, which is believed to be a divinely ordained constitutional and legal system. Moreover, because their political constituency in the north is at least nominally Muslim, these organizations fear the political consequences of openly opposing the application of Sharia. As a result, these intelligent and sensitive Muslim Sudanese are reduced to hiding behind the concerns and opposition of non-Muslim Sudanese instead of making their own original and credible challenge to the proponents of Sharia.

This complex and volatile situation was further complicated by the sudden and arbitrary imposition of Sharia in 1983 by former President Nimeiri. Let us therefore briefly review the background to this move and its impact on the national debate before resuming our discussion of the role of Islam in the Sudan.

Nimeiri's Legislative Coup of 1983

To understand why Nimeiri may have been prompted to take the drastic step of imposing Sharia as the public law of the Sudan in September 1983, we need to recall the beginnings and development of his regime, which came to power by means of a coup d'état on 25 May 1969.[35] One of the first steps that the new regime took was to seek a political settlement of the civil war in southern Sudan; this was eventually achieved through the Addis Ababa Agreement of 1972 and the establishment of regional autonomy for the southern region. Although the May regime had the initial support of the Sudanese Communist party, a power struggle soon ensued, ending in the defeat of the communists. The May regime now shifted its orientation to the center of Sudanese politics, and by 1973 it had enacted its own constitution and established a single-party state in the Sudan.

Because the traditional political forces in the country continued to oppose and actively sought to overthrow the May regime, Nimeiri attempted to develop his own independent political base in the country. He succeeded in gaining the political support both of southern Sudanese, whose confidence he had gained through his efforts to end the civil war and grant the southern region autonomous rule, and of a number of able intellectuals who were dissatisfied with the traditional political parties. Nevertheless, Nimeiri still felt insecure because of the continued political and military opposition to his regime by Sudanese political leaders operating from outside the Sudan. To neutralize that opposition, Nimeiri offered his adversaries, leaders of the Unionist and Umma parties and the Muslim Brothers, a chance to join him in what is known as the national reconciliation of 1977. The Unionists refused the offer, and the Umma party went along half-heartedly for a few months; but the Muslim Brothers took full advantage of the situation and managed to infiltrate all the political, legislative, and executive organs of the May regime. Nimeiri thus found himself pressed on both the internal and external fronts, with the Unionists and Umma forces opposing him from without and the Muslim Brothers undermining his authority from within his regime.

During the same period, Nimeiri is said to have had a personal religious experience that prompted him toward an Islamic approach to government. By the late 1970s, then, he started to express his preference for Islamic legislation and to introduce Islamic financial institutions throughout the country. The Muslim Brothers in the regime managed to manipulate this official Islamic policy as well, thereby consolidating their own political and economic positions.

In the meantime, political developments in the southern region were creating further problems for Nimeiri.[36] Some political forces there were demanding that the region be divided into three smaller regions, while others opposed such a move. At this point, Nimeiri took the initiative of dividing the southern region by presidential decree, without complying with the requirements of the constitution and the Addis Ababa Agreement. Within a few months of that decision, which cost him the support of most southern Sudanese, Nimeiri took the other drastic step of imposing Sharia, again by presidential decree, throughout the Sudan.

It is difficult to disentangle all these national, regional, and personal factors and place them in a scheme of cause and effect; in any case, they probably interacted with and reinforced one another in creating a severe crisis situation. The imposition of Sharia, in particular, seems to have been a desperate measure intended to gain political support from northern Muslims in order to counterbalance mounting political opposition from the south. The gamble failed, and Nimeiri was overthrown on 6 April 1985 while on an official visit to the United States.

Whatever Nimeiri's motives were for imposing Sharia by decree, that act introduced a wholly new element into the political situation. For the first time in the history of the modern Sudan, Sharia was the formal public law of the country. Overnight, the debate over the public role of Islam was transformed: the question now was not whether to implement Sharia, but whether to repeal it. This is the situation the Sudanese confronted during their third transitional stage.

Another consequence of Nimeiri's legislative action of 1983 was that it gave many Sudanese, Muslims and non-Muslims alike, a practical sense of what it means to live under Sharia as the public law of the land. While admittedly many of the judicial excesses and abuses that followed were due to the corruption and oppression of Nimeiri's regime as a whole, the experience has also demonstrated that Sharia itself is susceptible to manipulation and abuse. Indeed, the sweeping powers that Sharia allows the ruler and his representatives and its lack of constitutional and procedural safeguards make abuse and corruption unavoidable consequences of the modern application of Sharia.

With these two factors now firmly established in national politics, the Sudan found itself in another transitional stage. Will this transitional stage lead to the evolution of a just and workable constitution as the essential framework for national integration?

The Sudan in Transition, Again

The overthrow of Nimeiri in 1985 demonstrated, once again, the capacity of the Sudanese people to revolt, spontaneously and with little violence, against organized and armed oppression and corruption. More significantly, and despite (or perhaps because of) the existence of Sharia as the formal public law of the land, the transitional constitution of October 1985 embodied all the necessary principles of modern constitutionalism. In particular, the transitional constitution guaranteed complete freedom of religion and equality of all citizens before the law.[37]

Unfortunately, the transitional constitution also reflected the same old ambivalence toward Sharia. While providing for many principles that were either lacking in or openly inconsistent with Sharia, the transitional constitution made Sharia a main source of legislation.[38] Of course, provided that any legislation derived from Sharia was consistent with those constitutional provisions that guarantee equality before the law and nondiscrimination on grounds of religion, no serious objections could have been raised to this aspect of the constitution.

Moreover, the transitional stage was beset by other formidable problems for national integration. For one thing, the Sharia laws of 1983 remain the law of the land, still binding on the courts, which still implement them in their daily practice. Although the coalition parties in government failed to honor their campaign pledge to repeal those laws, they at least refused to execute any punishment of amputation. This particular executive policy, however, could be reversed at any time, in which case dozens of convicted persons will suffer amputations immediately.

A second major problem, clearly, is the continuation of the civil war in the south. Unlike the first cycle of the 1955–72 civil war, this time the declared objectives of the rebels are broader and their tactics and methods much more sophisticated. They are claiming to speak for all the disadvantaged peoples of the Sudan and seeking to establish a new order throughout the country.[39] In pursuit of their objectives, the rebels are organized politically as the Sudanese Peoples Liberation Movement (SPLM) and militarily as the Sudanese Peoples Liberation Army (SPLA). It remains to be seen how successfully these objectives can be achieved by the SPLM/SPLA through the available resources and whether those in charge will accept a transitional framework that may offer long-term rather than immediate achievement of their goals. For the time being, however, the SPLM/SPLA remains a formidable force in Sudanese politics.

For the purposes of the present discussion, the essential features of the transitional stage can be summarized as follows. First of all, no political party can claim genuine representation of all segments of the population throughout the country. Even the larger parties, namely the Umma and Unionist parties, and possibly the National Islamic Front, draw almost all their support from the northern Muslim population. Moreover, none of these parties can achieve enough parliamentary force to govern the country alone. Finally, even if any or all of these parties should unite, they cannot rule the whole country without the participation of the SPLM/SPLA in the south; conversely, the SPLM/SPLA requires the participation of the northern parties if it is to gain a ruling role.

When we look closely at the essential positions, rather than the rhetoric, of both sides to the national debate, we find that the northern parties are committed to Islam, while the southern forces are not necessarily opposed, provided the application of Islam does not violate the fundamental constitutional rights of non-Muslims as equal citizens of their own country. The real problem is that the generally held conception of Islam—namely, the public law of Sharia outlined above—*would* certainly violate their fundamental constitutional rights. In other words, so long as the northern parties remain committed to Sharia, there is no prospect for a resolution to the conflict and no chance for national integration.

Another, at least potential, political force is at work in the country, which may act to bring about a solution to the problem: namely, the educated and enlightened Sudanese from both parts of the country. At present, these individuals either are organized in small political parties and loose organizations, such as the Communist party and the Alliance of the Forces of the Uprising, or remain in the major parties but without true commitment to the fundamental nature and positions of those parties. Should these forces unite in pursuing a middle ground between the two main sides of the national debate, a solution to the problem of national integration may be worked out.

Reflections and Prospects

As I see it, the present deadlock is due to the fact that the main Muslim political parties are committed to Sharia as the only valid interpretation of Islam, whereas the non-Muslim political parties and organizations are opposed to Sharia because they know, or at least suspect, that its application would have drastic consequences for them. But is Sharia the only valid interpretation of Islam today?

To begin answering this question, let us recall two general points made in the opening paragraphs of this paper. First, because a monotheistic creed excludes nonbelievers, if it is made the basis of a constitutional and legal system, as in Sharia, nonbelievers will become subject peoples rather than citizens. Second, efforts to make a monotheistic creed the basis of the political and legal order have only succeeded in producing untold suffering throughout history. Both of these points have been amply demonstrated by the recent history of and present situation in the Sudan.

Paradoxically, the Sudan may also be the best candidate for the articulation and implementation of the Islamic reformation, for three main reasons. First, islamization in the now predominantly Muslim northern Sudan has always emphasized the values of toleration and peaceful coexistence. Despite recent tragic developments, a monotheistic Islamic state under strict Sharia has been an aberration and exception to the norm of moderation and tolerance in the Sudan.

Second, the country's current religious composition creates a good balance between the push toward the ideal of the *umma* under Sharia and the pull toward multireligious coexistence. In other words, whereas the Muslim population of the Sudan is strong enough to maintain its commitment to an Islamic ideal, the non-Muslim population is strong enough to resist the application of Sharia in its historical formulation without forcing the Muslims to abandon their Islamic ideal altogether.

The third reason for the suitability of the Sudan as a pioneer in Islamic reformation is the fact that such reformation has already been proposed and advocated by a Sudanese Muslim, namely the late Ustadh Mahmoud Mohamed Taha. Despite strong resistance by some traditional and "fundamentalist" Islamic groups in the country, the ideas of Ustadh Mahmoud are widely known throughout the country and respected by many Sudanese. Indeed, the current deadlock over the public role of Islam in Sudanese life may eventually recommend the approach proposed by Ustadh Mahmoud for redefining the Islamic ideal, thereby opening the way for genuine and lasting national integration in the country.

According to Ustadh Mahmoud, Islam consists of two overlapping messages, an eternal and universal one of complete justice and equality for all human beings without distinction as to race, creed, or gender, and a transitional message of relative justice among believers in terms of the quality of their belief.[40] He argued that the public law of Sharia is the transitional message, which by now has served its purpose; it must be superseded by the eternal and universal message, the practical implementation of which has, thus far, been precluded by the realities of human existence. Whereas the public law of Sharia was appropriate for the previous stages of human society, it is no longer appropriate and must make way for another version of the public law of Islam.

Although Ustadh Mahmoud was a Sudanese intellectual of impeccable character and integrity who advocated his views openly and peacefully for over thirty years, he was executed in the Sudan on 18 January 1985 for maintaining that position.[41] Moreover, despite active advocacy of his ideas, his hard-core following was of limited extent.

Neither of these facts is surprising, nor should they inspire despondence and despair over the success of his cause. Because he posed a major threat to the vested interests of forces within the Muslim population, he was bound to arouse hostility and violent reaction. And given the extraordinary nature of his views, it would have been surprising if he had gained a wide following in the short term.

Furthermore, despair is inappropriate for two reasons. First, his novel interpretation of Islam offers a perfect solution to the present crisis, in that it gives both sides what they want. To the Muslims, its gives a workable Islamic model that would satisfy their religious duty to live in accordance with the dictates of the Qur'an and Sunna; to non-Muslims, it gives a version of Islamic public law that would fully guarantee their fundamental constitutional rights as equal citizens of their own country. Second, even though his hard-core following was limited, he did enjoy very wide sympathy among educated and enlightened Sudanese.

In the end, any realistic hope for national integration in the Sudan requires that educated and enlightened Sudanese rise to the challenge of not only facing the proponents of Sharia with the unworkability of their model, but also proposing a viable Islamic alternative, such as that proposed by Ustadh Mahmoud. It is imperative to provide an Islamic alternative for the Muslim majority because, for them, Islam must have a role in public life. It is equally imperative to confront the proponents of Sharia with the inadequacy of their model because it will never permit national integration, which is the essential prerequisite for political stability, national security, and social and economic development. This paper does not purport to address all the questions and issues of national integration in the Sudan; rather, the objective is to address the specific issue of the application of historical Islamic Sharia as the public law of the Sudan. Because Islam is one of the most important forces affecting public life in the Sudan, the role of this religion must be defined in such a way as to increase the prospects of national integration in that country. Needless to say, many other problems, such as gross disparities in economic development, education, and other essential infrastructural components, must be resolved if true national integration is to be achieved. National integration is a long, delicate process that requires visionary statesmanship on the part of leaders and goodwill and patience on the part of the general population. Yet if any of these and other efforts and requirements are to have their desired effect of enhancing national integration, an appropriate constitutional and legal framework will have to be established in the country as a whole. It is my hope that this paper would contribute to the establishment of such a framework.

Postscript

As this paper was being prepared for publication, the military again seized power in the Sudan on 30 June 1989. The new military junta has abrogated the 1985 transitional constitution, dissolved the Constituent Assembly and the broad coalition headed by former Prime Minister Sadiq al-Mahdi, and banned all political parties and trade unions. It also canceled the licenses of all newspapers, partisan and "independent" alike, and took complete control of the media. What are the implications of these recent developments for the preceding discussion?

The declared objectives of the new regime include a final peaceful resolution of the security situation, especially in the western Sudan, the eradication of all corruption in political life and the civil service, and so forth. We need not elaborate on the reasons behind the coup, except to note that the Sudanese public seems generally to agree on the total failure of civilian governments since 1956 to address any of the country's economic and politicaproblems. I was in the Sudan during the several weeks immediately following the coup and found that most Sudanese, including professional and trade union leaders, perceive this development as an urgently needed relief from the utter incompetence and corruption of the leaders of the traditional political parties.

Nevertheless, there seems to be general skepticism as to the ability of the new junta to achieve their declared objectives. In particular, it is said that the new regime cannot end the civil war in the south and provide a lasting peaceful settlement of the southern problem. In my view, there are good grounds for this skepticism, especially in relation to the civil war and the so-called southern problem. In regard to the thorny issue of the role to be played by Sharia, which I believe to be the inevitable first step in any resolution process, the leaders of the new regime have declared that it would be solved through negotiations or, failing that, through a national referendum.

This latter solution, however, is neither practicable nor acceptable. It is not practicable because the security situation, especially in the south, would not permit the conduct of a national referendum. More importantly, the state of emergency imposed by the new regime and the absence of guarantees and mechanics for a genuinely free debate over the issue would make it impossible to conduct a *valid* referendum. In any case, the matter is too fundamental to be settled by the will of the majority. Given the clear preponderance of Muslims in the Sudan and their strong reverence for the Sharia, the vote in a referendum would most probably be in favor of upholding the application of Sharia throughout the country. Yet on this matter, the non-Muslim minority would likely not submit to the will of the majority. Nor should they, regardless of the size of the majority supporting such a policy. How can the will of the majority deny the minority their fundamental rights as equal citizens in their own country?

Unless the new regime changes its position on these issues, it may, at best, succeed in introducing an element of temporary relief in the security and supply of essential goods situations in the Sudan, but it will be unlikely to end the civil war and achieve a peaceful and lasting settlement of the southern problem. Without

that essential precondition, political stability, economic development, and the pursuit of national unity and integration are simply
unattainable.

Notes

1 Noel J. Coulson, *A History of Islamic Law* (Edinburgh, 1964), 120.

2 Joseph Schacht, *The Origins of Muhammadan Jurisprudence* (Oxford, 1959), 84.

3 S.G. Vesey-Fitzgerald, "Nature and Sources of the Shari'a," in Majid Khadduri and Herbert J. Liebesny (eds.), *Law in the Middle East* (Washington, D.C., 1955), 91.

4 See, generally, James P. Piscatori, *Islam in a World of Nation-States* (Cambridge, 1986).

5 Fazlur Rahman, *Islam* (Chicago, 1979), 229.

6 Rupert Emerson, *From Empire to Nation: The Rise to Self-Determination of Asian and African Peoples* (Cambridge, Mass., 1960), 89.

7 See, generally, Boyd C. Shafer, *Nationalism: Myth and Reality* (New York, 1955).

8 Emerson, *From Empire to Nation*, 91.

9 Ibid., 90–91.

10 Ibid., 95.

11 Ibid., 96.

12 Ibid.,97.

13 Yusuf Fadl Hassan, "Sudan Between the Fifteenth and Eighteenth Centuries," in Yusuf Fadl Hassan (ed.), *Sudan in Africa* (Khartoum, 1971), 76.

14 John Voll, "Renewal and Reform in Islamic History: *Tajdīd* and *Iṣlāḥ*," in John L. Esposito (ed.), *Voices of Resurgent Islam* (Oxford, 1983), 41.

15 R.S. O'Fahey and J.L. Spaulding, *Kingdoms of the Sudan* (London, 1974), 17.

16 See, generally, Jay Spaulding, *The Heroic Age in Sinnar* (Lansing, Michigan, 1985), pt. 1.

17 On this period of Sudanese history, see, generally, Richard Hill, *Egypt in the Sudan* (London, 1959).

18 See, generally, P.M. Holt, *The Mahdist State in the Sudan, 1881–1898* (Oxford, 1958); and A.B. Theobold, *The Mahdiyya* (London, 1951).

19 See, generally, Coulson, *History of Islamic Law*; and Schacht, *Origins of Muhammadan Jurisprudence*.

20 *Al-Muṣ'ḥaf* is generally accepted by Muslims as the accurate record of the Qur'an, though there may be room for debate on the subject; see John Burton, *The Collection of the Qur'an* (Cambridge, 1977), chap. 5. On the controversy over the Sunna, see Coulson, *History of Islamic Law*, 42; Rahman, *Islam*, 59–63; Vesey-Fitzgerald, "Nature and Sources of the Shari'a," 93.

21 Coulson, *History of Islamic Law*, 47–51; Kemal Faruki, *Islamic Jurisprudence* (Karachi, 1975), 166–94.

22 See, generally, H.A.R. Gibb,"Constitutional Organization," in Khadduri and Liebesny, *Law in the Middle East*; K. Faruki, *The Evolution of Islamic*

Constitutional Theory and Practice from 610 *to* 1926 (Karachi, 1971), 16–23.

23 For an account of the selection and appointment of the caliphs of Medina, see T.W. Arnold, *The Caliphate* (New York, 1966), 19–22.

24 Gibb, "Constitutional Organization," 17; Noel Coulson, "The State and the Individual in Islamic Law," *International and Comparative Law Quarterly* 6 (1957): 50–52, 57.

25 Majid Khadduri, *War and Peace in the Law of Islam* (Baltimore, 1955), 177, 195–199; *Encyclopedia of Islam* (new ed.)(Leiden, underway), 2:227.

26 Khadduri, *War and Peace in the Law of Islam*, 198; S.D. Goitein, "Minority Self-Rule and Government in Islam," *Studia Islamica* 31 (1970): 101–16. As pointed out in the *Encyclopedia of Islam* 2: 228–29, however, this doctrinal view of Sharia was not always maintained in practice because the administrative and bureaucratic abilities of *dhimmīs* were often needed by Muslim rulers.

27 Khadduri, *War and Peace in the Law of Islam*, 163–69.

28 On the definitions and technical requirements of these offenses, see generally Mohamed S. El-Awa, *Punishment in Islamic Law* (Indianapolis, 1982).

29 Safia Safwat, "Offenses and Penalties in Islamic Law," *Islamic Quarterly* 26 (1982): 175.

30 Coulson, "State and Individual in Islamic Law," 54–55.

31 Al-Shāfi'ī, *Kitāb al-umm* (Cairo, 1961), vi, 105–6.

32 'Abd al-Qādir 'Awda, *al-Tashrī' al-janā'ī al-islāmī* (Cairo, 1951), pars. 440, 535, 571, 618, 637.

33 Examples can be found in the writings of Dr. Hassan Aballa al-Turabi, the leader of the Islamic Front since 1964. See, too, Hassan al-Turabi, "The Islamic State," in Esposito, *Voices of Resurgent Islam*, 241–51.

34 Such opposition was voiced strongly in 1983 and 1984 when former President Nimeiri imposed Sharia throughout the country. See, for example, the statement of Sudanese Christian leaders published in *Origins* 14 (1986): 180-81 (National Catholic News Service, Washington, D.C.); and *Mashrek International*, February 1985, 28–30.

35 See, generally, John L. Esposito, "Sudan's Islamic Experiment," *Muslim World* 76 (1986): 181; and Khalid Duran, "The Centrifugal Forces of Religion in Sudanese Politics," *Orient* 26 (1985): 572.

36 On this dimension, see Ann Mosely Lesch, "Rebellion in the Southern Sudan," *Universities Field Staff International Reports* 12, no. 8 (Africa [AML-1-1985]).

37 Arts. 17 and 18 of the transitional constitution of 1985.

38 Art. 4 of the transitional constitution of 1985.

39 Lesch, "Rebellion in the Southern Sudan," 11–14.

40 For a good statement of Ustadh Mahmoud's position and arguments, see Mahmoud Mohamed Taha, *The Second Message of Islam* (Syracuse, N.Y., 1987).

41 On the circumstances of the trial and execution of Ustadh Mahmoud, see Abdullahi A. An-Na'im, "The Islamic Law of Apostasy and Its Modern Applicability: A Case from the Sudan," *Religion* 16 (1986): 197.

A Three-Dimensional Approach to the
Conflict in the Sudan   FRANCIS M. DENG

This paper is a short account of some of the work I have done over the last several years with respect to the current conflict in the Sudan, centering largely on three interrelated sets of activities. One concerns a sociohistorical analysis of Sudan's identity crisis behind the conflict; the second covers two works of fiction in which I try to substantiate the theme of identity crisis in narrative form; and the third relates to the role of participant-observer in a peace process that I initiated jointly with Gen. Olusegun Obasanjo, former head of state of Nigeria, in 1987, a role that entailed facilitating communication between the conflicting parties, learning more about the conflict, and attempting to bridge the differences. To place these concerns in perspective, let us briefly consider the conflict and its geopolitical context.

Background

As the Sudan approached its independence on 1 January 1956, there was considerable international optimism about the role it was destined to play, not only in linking sub-Saharan Africa with the Arab Muslim countries to the north, but also in forming a bridge between Africa and the Middle East. Geographically the largest country in Africa, the Sudan abuts eight sub-Saharan and north African countries: Egypt, Ethiopia, Kenya, Uganda, Zaire,

The original version of this paper was first presented at the U.S. Institute of Peace as "Work in Progress" during my term there as Jennings Randolph Distinguished Fellow.

Central African Republic, Chad, and Libya. Because all the ethnic and cultural diversities of these countries are reflected within Sudan's borders, the country is an Afro-Arab microcosm. Postulating the international role of his country in Arab-African terms, the foreign minister of the newly independent Sudan observed: "The Sudan is, in the main, a cognate part of the Arab world and this is why we hastened to join the Arab League immediately on the declaration of our independence. . . . Our relations with the Arab countries will not make us lose sight of our African ties of affinity. We will always look south to Africa, strengthening our relations with the different African peoples and trying to help them in their progress and evolution towards freedom and a better life." Outsiders echoed the same views. The U.S. Department of State welcomed the Sudanese aspiration for intermediacy: "As a new African nation, the Sudan will be deeply involved in [the] future cause of Africa. But as a Middle Eastern nation, too, the Sudan will also be a bridge to Africa, imparting to it ideas, philosophies, and forces which may have great influence on Africa's decisions and on its future."

Since 1955, several months before the declaration of independence, however, the Sudan has suffered a chronic domestic conflict, punctuated between 1972 and 1983 by a precarious peace accord. While the issues involved are complex and multifaceted, the central theme in the conflict is the north-south religious, racial, and cultural dichotomy, with its attendant disparities or inequities in the shaping and sharing of power, wealth, and other values. The north, two-thirds of the country in land and population, is Islamic and arabized. Generally speaking, it has also benefited more than the south from opportunities for political, economic, social, and cultural development, especially through colonial intervention. The south, which constitutes the remaining third in both land and population, is more indigenously African in religion, race, and culture and, except for a small, educated, predominantly Christian minority, has hardly benefited from socioeconomic development. These inequities and the resulting fears of northern domination in an independent Sudan triggered the mutiny of a southern battalion that later escalated into the seventeen-year civil war.

The conflict has been the principal source of instability in post-colonial Sudan, leading to a succession of civilian governments, two military dictatorships, and two popular uprisings that over-threw those military governments and restored parliamentary democracy. Paradoxically, the conflict continues to threaten the democracy for which the Sudanese people have repeatedly demonstrated their commitment.

Identity

Although the war that has raged in the southern part of the Sudan since the dawn of independence has several interacting dimen-sions, the issue of national identity has perhaps emerged as the pivotal factor, with the north perceived as striving to structure the country in its Arab Islamic image and the south seen as resisting the northern attempt to dominate and assimilate the south. The identity factor raises several sets of interrelated questions: What are the identities of the parties in the conflict? To what extent is the war in fact a conflict of identities between the Arab north and the African south? How justified is the south-north dichotomy on racial and cultural grounds? More substantially, what is the con-flict all about? In particular, what are the complications of identi-ty demarcation in terms of who gets what from the system, and why has religion become a dominant factor in the conflict? Final-ly, what alternative avenues exist given the identity dimension of the conflict and its implications for the shaping and sharing of values?

To appreciate the pivotal role of religion in the conflict, it should be remembered that Islam welds together all aspects of life, public and private, into a composite whole that is ideally regulat-ed by Sharia. Although traditional religions of the south also fol-low an integrated approach to life, their system is based on an autonomous hierarchy in which the sanctions of God and spiritu-al powers are exercised through a segmentary lineage system that ensures some form of contextual relativity and freedom in religious matters. The Christianized southerners, being the products of an educational system oriented to the West, not only are alienated from the religious traditions of their people, but are also predisposed to resist an Islamic theocracy and favor the separation of religion and the state.

A close examination of the historical process by which these competing and now conflicting identities were shaped, the manner in which power and national resources have been disproportionately allocated along these identity lines, and the reaction to these inequities among the disadvantaged highlight several points about the identity issue underlying the conflict. First, the historical process that shaped the contemporary Sudanese scene has given communities in all regions of the country layers of multiple identities that defy monolithic labels. The Sudan—both north and south—has been influenced over the centuries both by indigenous African religions and by Judaism, Christianity, and Islam. These composite identities tend to be oversimplified by claims of allegedly "pure" religious, racial, and cultural identities, misperceptions that clearly misrepresent and distort the realities of the Sudan.

Second, judging from the history of islamization and arabization in the north and of southern resistance to Arab-Islamic assimilation, it would seem that the prospects for integration are considerably enhanced by persuasion rather than by coercion. When the environment is conducive to peaceful interaction between religions, races, and cultures, a process of give-and-take occurs in which what is accepted or rejected is likely to be determined by the objective advantages or disadvantages accruing from affiliation into a given identity. It could indeed be argued that resistance to assimilation increases in direct proportion to the level of coercion applied.

Third, unlike other black African countries such as Mali, Nigeria, Senegal, or Sierra Leone, where Muslims are the majority of the population, in the Sudan Islamic identity has, for historical and geographical reasons, been intimately associated with Arab racial and cultural identification. This association has in turn deepened the racial and cultural dichotomy between the north and the south.

Several policy questions emanate from these points. First, given that misperceptions about identity have produced divisive myths that obscure the racial and cultural realities of the Sudan, could removing the myths and revealing the realities provide a common denominator on which to build a more uniting sense of national identity and collective purpose? Assuming an affirmative answer, it could be argued that quite apart from any constitutional, political, and administrative arrangements that might be adopted to expedite realization of this goal, the process of national self-discovery is essentially a function of education, broadly defined. Thus, it could also be argued that while the leadership might accelerate the speed of progress, there can be no significant short-cuts, and it would inevitably take a considerable amount of time to correct the mistakes of the past. Conversely, it could be argued that what should count is what people believe they are, not what they are in fact. To attempt to deny the majority their perceived identity may be as objectionable as attempting to impose on the minority the majority perceptions of national identity. Viewed from the opposite side, why should the minority be expected to invest valuable time in attempting to change the perceptions of those who believe in a particular identity? Should they not deal with the majority group on the basis of that perceived identity?

A second policy question arising from the history of arabization and islamization in the Sudan, including resistance to Arab-Islamic assimilation in the south, is whether the chances of success might be maximized by persuasion rather than coercion, no matter what religious, racial, or cultural mold one favors in the formulation of a national identity.

The third question is whether in a country as religiously, racially, and culturally diverse as the Sudan it would be politically prudent or even realistic to build the national character around the identity of any one group.

If my assumptions about the identity factor in the conflict are correct, how is the problem of competing and conflicting identities, with their religious overtones, likely to be resolved? Three possible options could be speculated upon. The first two are rather extreme and, in my opinion, undesirable; the third is, I believe, more practical and appealing.

The first option is for the Arab-Islamic position to prevail through decisive military victory that would permit the north to fashion the country along theocratic lines. Despite the proselytizing zeal of the Muslim fundamentalists, the vast financial resources of the Arab-Islamic world, and the Arab global influence, it is highly unlikely that this scenario could succeed.

Should the Islamic faction fail to achieve its objectives militarily, the second option is separation. If the south were simply let go of, the north would be free to build an Islamic state unhampered by southern resistance—a course the Islamic fundamentalists might favor. This option presupposes a separatist predisposition on the part of the south, something that can no longer be taken for granted, for the southern position on the issues of unity and separatism has over time grown increasingly complex. The leadership of the Sudan Peoples Liberation Army (SPLA) and its political wing, the Sudan Peoples Liberation Movement (SPLM), have stipulated as their goal the liberation of the whole country from any form of discrimination. Nevertheless, it is common knowledge that the aspiration of the fighting men is largely regional and is aimed at ridding the south of northern Arab-Islamic domination, real or perceived. While the SPLM/SPLA leadership may view the liberation of the south as inextricably tied to changing the national identity and power structure at the center, the view of the rank and file—a view discreetly shared by the overwhelming majority of the educated civilian elite—is that separatism, if achievable, would be the simplest solution. Quite apart from the objective merits of unity, however, the regional African and international climate simply would not favor separatism, as everyone realizes. Indeed, the SPLM/SPLA position is cynically viewed by some as a clever ploy to conceal their separatist intentions in order to neutralize opposition to separatism and facilitate the attainment of their hidden agenda. If the north were sincerely to want separatism, then the obstacles to that end would be considerably reduced.

But what if the SPLM/SPLA is serious about its declared objective of pursuing national unity and liberating the whole country from all forms of discrimination? It is generally recognized that they cannot impose their will by military means on the whole nation; the most they can be expected to do, then, is resist the imposition of Islamic theocracy on the nation and block partition.

The third option, which strikes me as most practical under the prevailing circumstances, would be some form of compromise that would apply the three policy implications of the identity themes: remove the divisive myths from the debate on national identity, establish a peaceful national environment, and build the nation on institutionalized unity in diversity. In other words, what is likely to work is a system that would accommodate separatism within unity through a confederation or federation. Such a system would, it is to be hoped, create an atmosphere of harmonious coexistence and interaction that could permit a gradual process of integration and an evolution of a genuinely uniting national identity. The result might be appropriately called Sudanese, Afro-Arab, or Arab-African rather than either Arab or African.

The question of which alternative will eventually prevail depends on a number of unpredictable regional and international variables. It is however obvious that while the challenges of unity are formidable, the problems of separatism for both north and south are even more overwhelming. Unity thus becomes not only a desirable goal, but a national imperative.

The forces of moderation in both parts of the country, thus, are the only hope in shaping a unifying national character: forces that do not favor a theocratic state, are committed to a concept of national unity on the basis of equitable diversity, and are prepared to postulate and foster a radical transformation of the country along those lines. An enlightened, progressive, charismatic leadership with the vision and the persuasive power to win popular support through the democratic process holds the key. But if democracy fails to accomplish this pressing national goal, yet another military takeover could, paradoxically, ensue.

Narrative

If I am correct about what underlies much of the conflict and how it might be resolved, then one of the ways of approaching the conflict and the problem of its resolution is to change the consciousness of the people. After leaving public life and pondering what in practical terms I might do, in addition to scholarly study, to address the pressing problems of my country, I thought that a better means of reaching the popular consciousness where the myths of identity tend to take hold might be a story, rather than a historical or political analysis aimed at an intellectual elite. It is in this context that my two novels, *Seed of Redemption* and *Cry of the Owl*, should be viewed. These stories are in effect attempts to communicate the themes of identity formation, their mythical foundations, and their policy implications to the Sudanese readership so as to neutralize divisive myths and shed light on unifying realities. Although they are loosely described as novels, their didactic nature and analytical orientation distinguish them from the standard Western novel form.

Seed of Redemption (New York, 1986) was well received in scholarly circles abroad and, as I had hoped, has provoked a great deal of controversy in the Sudan. One American anthropologist wrote:

> *Seed of Redemption* . . . exposes and thus explodes the myth of a singular Arab identity in many Sudanese communities by show- ing how centuries of intermarriage (in the midst of perennial confrontations) have created a northern or "Arab" population ever conscious of denying real history. The central character of the novel, Faris–culturally a northerner but representing a southern heritage–is the living embodiment of each tradition. He emerges in the second half of the novel as the hope and promise of true unity and peace in the country.

A Sudanese historian and student of African literature cogently captured the spirit of the novel in a review that was published at home and abroad:

The hero of this intriguing novel is Faris Khalifa, a Sudanese army officer and a great grandson of a southern woman who had been taken slave late in the nineteenth century and spent the rest of her life in the North. His father was from Dar Fur in Western Sudan, while one of his grandfathers was an Egyptian. In Faris's veins, therefore, runs as much African blood as Arab. Culturally he is the personification of the Sudanese society; the natural product of centuries of intermarriage, intermixing and the cross-cultural interaction between Arabs and Africans that give the Sudanese people those distinctive characteristics of which they are proud. Because of his mixed heritage, his patriotism, and above all, in fulfillment of an ancestral prophecy, Faris is destined to play a pivotal role in the history of the Sudan, to salvage its unity after years of bloody civil wars in the south the causes of which go back to the early contacts between Northerners and Southerners. Convinced in the end that the policies of his unstable, born-again Muslim President, Jabir Munir, will ruin the Sudan, Faris ousts Munir from power and sets the stage for a new beginning, a new society free of prejudice and discrimination.

The potential of the novel in practical terms was underscored by the reviewer who wrote that, "as political-historical polemic," *Seed of Redemption* "must be taken very seriously indeed." And another reviewer wrote, "Deng has written a highly provocative novel and a valuable and unique addition to Sudanese literature. However, unless this important work is translated into Arabic, it will remain beyond the reach of the majority of the people about whom it has been written."

Cry of the Owl (New York, 1989) pursues that theme of identity crises in a more genuinely fictional form, and although it is still in press, it has received positive responses from readers. When I first began working on the story, I was still driven by the objective of exploding the myths of identity that artificially divide the Sudan into Arab north and African south. As the story unfolded, however, I found myself substantiating other phenomena, which, rather than detracting from the main theme or thesis, indicated a deepening of perspectives on the dynamics of Sudanese identity. For example, I began to realize, perhaps for the first time, that being a Dinka, much like being an Arab, is a function not only of blood, but also, and perhaps more importantly, of culture. A half-blood Dinka, or someone with no Dinka blood at all but raised a Dinka, could be as much Dinka as a full-blooded member of the group. The converse is also true: a full-blooded Dinka could be culturally and even racially disaffiliated from his Dinka environment and assimilated into another supposedly alien or foreign identity. Once the fiction exposed me to these dynamics, realities that I had only casually observed in some individuals from both the Dinka and the northern Arab contexts suddenly had a greater impact on my thinking. The criss-crossing on the racial and cultural dividing lines became clearer as elements of the ongoing process of shaping and institutionalizing personal and collective identities.

Another phenomenon that I fortuitously discovered through the story is the power of human interaction and its potential in reshaping and changing perceptions, including prejudices. One's initial outlook is of course shaped by the environment in which one finds oneself and the people with whom one interacts at the formative period in one's life. One therefore begins with preconceived ideas about others and shares collective prejudices with the group in which one is first socialized. As a result of exposure to individuals from "other" groups, however, one begins to recognize elements that belie the patterns assumed to define collective identities. Again, once the process of writing *Cry of the Owl* opened my eyes and sensitized me to this human phenomenon, I began to recall and see many instances of individual exceptions to the otherwise established perceptions and prejudices. Of course, exceptions are so often personalized that they can challenge the norms only on a very limited scale; what matters is how aware people are of these exceptions and their cumulative significance. Within the Sudanese context, such awareness, to the extent that it exists, is minimal and is relegated to a subconscious level that does not impact on relations across the dividing lines.

The result of these two contradictory phenomena of societal rigidities and individual flexibilities is a situation of extreme volatility. Myths can, of course, continue to be generated and transfused to reinforce and consolidate collective preconceptions. As part of that process, mutual assimilation of individuals on both sides is accepted and sometimes encouraged, with successes and failures in assimilating largely depending on the advantages and disadvantages associated with the identity concerned. The side that offers the greatest prospects for self-enhancement in terms of political, social, cultural, or economic standing naturally enjoys a better chance of assimilating. Whatever the equations of advantages and disadvantages across the dividing line, the result of heightened competition between identities is likely to be greater polarization with a hardening of positions and increased tensions and conflicts. In the case of the Sudan, the tragic irony is that the current confrontation is based largely on illusions translated into realities that now loom larger than life.

The positive alternative is for people to become increasingly aware of the deeper truth, unraveled through close examination of situations involving people less caught up in the distorted stereotypes of the collective identity. While initially this sensitizing experience may be rationalized on the grounds that individuals are mere exceptions to the rule, with the basis for the prejudice against the group as a whole remaining unaffected, as exceptions multiply they are bound to push more people from a stereotyped to a contextualized understanding of internal and cross-cultural complexities, including a more reliable appreciation of commonalities and differences. The process, although subtle, will, I believe, be unavoidably moderating in its impact.

The narrative form of communication could, indeed, make an effective, broad-based contribution to a better understanding of social issues and help promote the cause of peace in the Sudan. My faith in this regard was considerably enhanced by a personal letter I received from Professor Abdullahi An-Na'im, a highly respected Sudanese scholar of Islamic jurisprudence and a senior member of the Republican Brothers, an elite religious group that is endeavoring to reinterpret the message of Islam to be more in tune with the pluralism of the modern nation-state. This lofty goal cost their leader, Ustadh Mahmoud Mohamed Taha, his life: he was condemned and executed for apostasy under the so-called September Islamic laws of former President Gaafar Mohammed Nimeiri. Professor An-Na'im, the foremost disciple of the saintly Ustadh, has continued the message with the combined zest of scholar and activist. My publisher and I agreed that Professor An-Na'im's letter should form a preface to *Cry of the Owl*:

> It was an extremely enjoyable and instructive experience for me to read the manuscript of your novel, *Cry of the Owl*, last week-end. I found the manuscript so fascinating and provocative that I couldn't put it down or do anything else until I had finished reading it.
>
> Your earlier novel, *Seed of Redemption*, had already introduced me to the potential of the fiction form in addressing the complicated and sensitive issues of national unity and social transformation in the Sudan. I must admit that I have found *Cry of the Owl* much more effective as a tool for exposing and discussing the most sensitive and deep-rooted issues in our individual and collective psyche. In fact, I can now see a far-reaching and even revolutionary potential of the fiction method.
>
> Coming from the Ja'aliyn tribe of the northern central Sudan, known for their strong prejudice and shameful commercial exploitation of southern Sudanese since the days of the "institutionalized" slave trade, *Cry of the Owl* has succeeded in provoking deep emotions and reflections on my part. As you probably know from my short piece in *The Search for Peace and Unity in the Sudan*, I am of the view that all Sudanese must undergo the painful but extremely beneficial process of exposing deep-rooted prejudice and social discrimination before they can hope to evolve a genuine sense of national identity and achieve lasting peace and justice in the Sudan. Through *Cry of the Owl*, I have had a most revealing personal experience in practicing what I preach.
>
> For example, I have found that the most moving parts of the manuscript were those explaining and exploring Dinka culture. Besides confronting me with my shameful ignorance about this profound cultural tradition so close to home, I found myself deeply resonating with many aspects of that tradition. In reading your skillful exposition and illustration of that extremely rich and humane tradition, I came to a greater appreciation of what you mean when you

say that the so-called "animists" of the Sudan are as religious, if not more so, as the adherents of Islam and Christianity.

In terms of its immediate and profound contribution to re- solving our country's chronic state of instability and insecurity, I was particularly struck by the manuscript's skillful and very convincing analysis of the subtle elements of individual and collective self-identity. The manuscript's very clear exposition and analysis of the shifting and intricate ingredients and processes of identity, with their far-reaching practical implications, offer both diagnosis and treatment for some of the deep-rooted causes of conflict and tension in the Sudan.

For this novel to achieve its full potential, it must be translated into Arabic and widely distributed throughout the Sudan. As you know, the majority of our educated compatriots cannot read English well enough, and cannot afford novels published in English. A skillful and artistic Arabic translation, preferably prepared under your personal guidance and published locally in the Sudan, would make this wonderful novel available to people who need to read it most. Moreover, I wonder whether it is possible for this novel to reach, in some form, the vast majority of our population who are illiterate. I even dreamed of its production as a movie or television drama for broadcast in rural Sudan.

Peace Initiative

Another level at which the Sudan conflict can and is being addressed—one that could contribute, if only in a small way, toward education and changing the perceptions of the leaders—is in trying to foster mutual understanding between the conflicting groups and assist them in achieving an end to the war.

Since the popular uprising that overthrew the regime of Nimeiri in April 1985, the search for peace and unity has been a national preoccupation. Despite an apparently sincere yearning to end the war that has intermittently bedeviled the country since the dawn of independence, peace has continued to elude the Sudan. The transitional government that coached the country back to parliamentary democracy and the elected government of Prime Minister Sadiq al-Mahdi both made several overtures and approaches to the SPLM/SPLA, which in turn has consistently asserted its commitment to a negotiated settlement. Groups inside and outside the country, governments and individuals, have offered their good offices to facilitate the parties' desire for a peaceful settlement of the conflict. Important meetings and talks have taken place between representative groups and leaders of both sides. Nevertheless, no appreciable progress has been made toward peace; the need for continued efforts remains compelling.

It was against this background that Gen. Olusegun Obasanjo and I ventured a personal peace initiative in August 1987. Earlier that year, in February, a workshop on the conflict was held at the Woodrow Wilson International Center for Scholars in Washington, D.C., which, in addition to independent scholars, Sudanese representatives from both sides attended and to which we invited General Obasanjo. I had already, as minister of state for foreign affairs, had the good fortune of working with General Obasanjo on matters pertaining to regional peace and security in Africa and had been very much impressed by his dedication to the cause of peace, demonstrated by his placing substantive achievements above protocol formalities. The results of the workshop were published several months later in a book, produced in conjunction with the U.S. Institute of Peace, called *The Search for Peace and Unity in the Sudan*. General Obasanjo and I then agreed to use the book and the ideas generated by the workshop as a basis for exploratory discussions with leaders on both sides. The objective was to try to understand better the underlying issues, identify any misconceptions that might adversely affect the prospects for peace, and explore potential grounds for a settlement. Our initiative has entailed several visits to the Sudan and neighboring countries and has resulted in two substantive reports that have received encouraging responses from concerned governments, organizations, and individuals worldwide.

General Obasanjo brought our efforts to the attention of his colleagues in the InterAction Council of Former Heads of Government and State, a group of eminent world leaders who remain concerned with major world issues and have continued to wield considerable influence, despite having relinquished active power in their own countries. The policy board of the council decided to include the Sudanese conflict on the agenda for their meeting in Harare, Zimbabwe, on 19–20 March 1988. Both the Sudanese government and the SPLM/SPLA were invited, and they responded by sending high-level delegations, including leading members of all the major political parties. After considering the item, the board decided:

1. To appeal to both sides to continue efforts in search of a peaceful resolution of the conflict and, in particular, to promote dialogue and negotiation at the highest level.
2. To appeal to both sides to allow the delivery of badly needed food and other relief supplies to the starving and dying civilian population in the war-stricken south.
3. To support the efforts to promote dialogue undertaken by General Obasanjo and Dr. Francis Deng and, in particular, to encourage them to go a step further in identifying the issues, the positions of the parties on those issues, and alternative grounds for a peaceful solution.
4. To establish a small committee, to include, in addition to General Obasanjo and Dr. Francis Deng, Dr. Kurt Furgler, Mr. Pierre Trudeau, Dr. Manuel Ulloa, and Dr. Schimberni, to mobilize resources from the international community for wartime relief and postwar rehabilitation, reconstruction, and equitable development aimed at bridging the disparities that contributed greatly to the root causes of the conflict.

Our efforts also led to an agreement between the prime minister and the leader of the SPLM/SPLA to hold secret alks in Europe immediately following the Harare meeting. Unfortunately, a few days before the scheduled meeting, the SPLM/SPLA leader, John Garang, declined to attend for logistical reasons, alleging that he had not been fully consulted on the timing and venue and that he was too deep inside the southern sector to get to Europe at the specified time. Since we had been meticulous about keeping both sides in the picture, it would seem reasonable to assume that other factors must have figured in Garang's decision, although it is possible that he might not have been fully informed in time about the details.

For now, then, the peace process has slowed down. But the quest for peace and unity in the Sudan persists, and we remain committed to doing whatever we can to further that cause. At this juncture, we feel that we owe it to the Sudanese and all those who have seen us struggling to keep the process alive, as well as to those who have supported our initiative, morally or materially, to report on what we have so far tried to do, where things now stand, what we have learned, and what we see to be the future prospects for peace. Accordingly, we have prepared a book under the working title "Pursuing Peace in the Sudan," which includes a report on the initial contacts with both sides, followed by successive reports on several activities pertaining to the peace process: the Washington workshop, our first joint initiative, our followup visit, the consideration of the issue by the InterAction Council of Former Heads of State and Government, and the meeting that was to have taken place between the prime minister and Garang. We conclude the book with a brief review of prospects for the future and a series of documents pertaining to the peace process. In addition, Professor William Zartman of the School of Advanced International Studies, Johns Hopkins University, in an extensive introduction, places our narrative into a broader, analytical framework with respect to the theory and practice of conflict resolution.

Let me highlight some of the main aspects of the conflict that we had hoped the parties would consider had they met, and that we have outlined in the book: the overriding goals of the parties, the substantive issues they agreed to discuss, and the various considerations that we believe would have influenced their evaluation and choice of options.

Mutual Objectives of the Parties

The leaders on both sides of the conflict explicitly avowed three principal objectives: the preservation of national unity within the geographic Sudan; ongoing dialogue and the search for peaceful alternatives to armed conflict; and the creation of a new Sudan in which all citizens would enjoy a sense of belonging and genuine equality. Because these were goals, naturally the parties differed on just how they should be interpreted and on ways of pursuing them. Furthermore, these goals could not all be attained at the same pace or to the same degree; while some might be achieved relatively rapidly, others would necessitate stages of laying down the principles necessary to permit progress toward the desired objectives.

Specific Issues

With respect to the specific issues for discussion, the challenge facing the leaders was to formulate the broad outlines of the new Sudan and the bases on which they would be prepared to agree. Particular factors included: the constitutional framework and political arrangements that would ensure equitable partici-pation on the local, regional, and national levels; the relationship between religion and the state, a central issue in the constitutional debate currently under way in the country; security arrangements between the regional and central governments, arrangements crit-ical to the balance of power and the stability of any system of gov-ernment that might be agreed upon; national identity, one of the most controversial and preoccupying concerns in the national debate; economic considerations, particularly arrangements for an equitable sharing of national wealth and balanced develop-ment; cultural matters, of which language and the educational system are the most (though by no means the only) critical fac-tors; and foreign policy, especially as it relates to surrounding states and regional organizations and, in particular, cooperation between the Sudan and neighboring countries in effecting the peaceful resolution of internal and regional conflicts in those countries.

Factors Favoring Talks

Among the major factors of the conflict situation that the leadership on both sides would have had to consider in contem-plating a peaceful resolution were the following: first, that the war was not winnable by either side; second, that the escalation of the conflict and its increasing internationalization meant that the time might soon come when the Sudanese, including the leadership, would lose control of the situation and look to external actors to decide the destiny of their country; and third, that the people of the Sudan were likely to be driven by severe suffering to extreme courses of action, ones antithetical to the demonstrated Sudanese yearning for democracy and consequently to the detriment of current leadership.

Parameters of a Settlement
The book also attempts to outline an acceptable settlement of the conflict. Assuming the parties agreed that an urgent peaceful resolution of the conflict was imperative, what might the overall parameters of a settlement be? Certainly no settlement would be acceptable that did not cater to the most vital concerns and interests of the other party. Also, a successful settlement would have to leave both sides feeling that they had gained appreciably and not lost unduly. For any solution to succeed, moreover, due consideration would have to be given to public opinion: the solution would have to be entertained by the bulk of the Sudanese people who had persistently demonstrated their commitment to democracy. Taking into consideration the vital concerns and interests of both sides would mean, as far as the national leadership is concerned, that no solution that might force them out of office would be negotiable. From the perspective of the SPLM/SPLA leadership, no solution that did not significantly satisfy the aspirations of the movement and in particular the fighting men would be acceptable. Finally, from the national perspective, it would be imperative that the solution be seen to benefit all the regions and people of the Sudan, and not only the area that had taken up arms.

A Possible Way Out

What particular solution could both recognize the power of the current rulers and meet the aspirations of the SPLM/SPLA to an acceptable degree? Here, we turned to the declared objectives of the SPLM/SPLA and the constraints to their realization. The movement had declared that it was fighting for the liberation of the whole country, but most Sudanese, including the leaders of the movement themselves, recognized that they could not over-run the country and seize the reins of national government by force. We also became convinced that the real motivation for fighting, as far as the rank and file in the south was concerned, had to do with regional aspirations and liberation from central domination, real or perceived, rather than the so-called liberation of the whole country. This led to an important unappreciated insight: whereas the leadership stressed national unity, thus appealing to public opinion inside the Sudan and in Africa, the grass-root objective of the movement was to control regional power within the framework of one country, with an equitable sharing of national power. Nevertheless, the issue should not be seen as merely a balancing of the power of the current rulers with the aspirations of the movement and the fighting men; the two had to be perceived in terms of a collective vision that was accept-able to the nation as a whole.

The above analysis suggested to us that an agreement was possi-ble along certain lines. First, a political recognition of the SPLM/SPLA by the government in the context of both regional and national aspirations was necessary, balanced by the move-ment's recognition of the government as democratically elected. Second, both sides had to pledge to cooperate in the creation of a unified new Sudan. And third, in conjunction with the correction of past inequities in the interest of freedom, justice, and unity, it was vitally important to cater to the collective interest of the Sudanese people as a whole.

Both parties needed to agree on several fundamental guidelines for the creation of the new Sudan, including: (1) the adoption of a balanced structure that would give the people of each region full political and economic control over the affairs of their re-gion within the framework of national unity, thereby enabl-ing each region to adopt any legislation appropriate to its social, cultural, and religious environment; (2) the formulation of principles that would ensure equality among all citizens irrespective of race, religion, or gender; (3) an invitation to the leadership of the SPLM/SPLA to participate in the regional and national governments, in full consultation with the internal political forces; (4) the mobilization of international cooperation in the postwar challenge of repatriation, rehabilitation, reconstruction, and development of the country, in particular the most affected or neglected areas; and (5) the formulation of basic foreign policy, especially principles that the Sudan might adopt in relations with its neighbors to foster bilateral cooperation in the peaceful settlement of internal and regional disputes.

Implementation

Assuming that the parties reached an agreement, they would still face a formidable challenge in winning the support of their respective constituencies and political allies. Under such circumstances, it would be strategically prudent to allow, within the commitment to broad principles, sufficient scope for the discussion and formulation of details. A program of action might be designed along the following lines: first, a joint declaration of the broad principles of the agreement reached, leaving room for each side to present details as appropriate to its own political context; second, the formation of an All-Party Committee to consider the principles of the agreement in greater depth and to prepare for the constitutional conference; third, the announcement of a cease-fire and the lifting of the emergency; fourth, the convening of a conference to draft the constitution; fifth, the formation of a government of national unity to oversee the election of a constituent assembly; sixth, the final drafting and adoption of the constitution by the Constituent Assembly; and seventh, declaration of the new Sudan.

These, then, were some of the conclusions we derived from the process and that we hoped might provide a basis for further discussions among the conflicting groups and other interested parties. Although the intended meeting was to be bilateral and strictly confidential, a few mediators—honest brokers, men of good will toward both sides—would have been available to facilitate the parties' progress toward their desired objective. The parties were to decide those people's role: whether they should remain outside the meetings but be available on demand, or whether they should participate directly in the discussions.

It would be wrong and impertinent to presume anything about the prospects of the meeting. Indeed, subsequent developments, including the formation of a government by dominant northern political forces, all united by Islam and Arabism, indicate that much groundwork for a potential agreement is still necessary. Had the meeting occurred, however, it might well have pushed the peace process forward; its failure to be held, I believe, should be counted as a setback in the peace process.

Broader Lessons

Our peace initiative was a learning process for us and the leaders on both sides. We certainly deepened our understanding of the conflict as seen by the two parties, and perhaps we helped the leaders gain a better understanding of the issues from their different perspectives. In retrospect, I realize that I learned a valuable lesson from this experience, one that my other experiences with third-party involvement would tend to confirm: namely, there is a delicate balance between being a discrete facilitator of the parties' own intentions and interactions and being an initiator whose influence and effectiveness lie in shedding light on new angles and possibilities, always with optimal mutual interest as the desired end result. The function is perhaps comparable to being behind the class, learning from observation, spotlighting from the rear what might otherwise not be apparent, and occasionally stepping forward to explain and argue. When there is no other leverage, whether through threats of sanctions or promises of rewards, only the wisdom of the words remains the vital tool of influence. Such wisdom need not be glaringly obvious. Sometimes even a rhetorical question can have the desired effect. On one occasion, for example, after explaining to the prime minister the position that the leader of the SPLM/SPLA enjoyed—that is, not only as chairman of the movement, but also as commander-in-chief of a sizable and well-equipped army, whose leadership was recognized by an increasing number of African leaders—I asked him what he could possibly offer Garang to make peace more attractive than his present position and what could satisfy both him, Garang, and his men so that they would follow him into peace rather than rebel and select another leader. Conversely, I asked the prime minister how much he could afford to offer without endangering his own constituency. I also asked both the prime minister and Garang how they envisaged agreeing and joining hands when they were leaders of systems that were fundamentally at variance, one a democracy and the other an armed struggle. The answers we got to these questions provided us with the most tangible evidence of potential bases for a settlement.

Obviously, more reflection on experiences in the field and a more disciplined and comparative analysis of the entire situation would be required before it could be ascertained whether the principles of conflict resolution that General Obasanjo and I developed are universally valid or context-specific and to what extent the cultural dimension is relevant. In any event, it would seem reasonable to assume that when managing or resolving disputes people apply principles that are in tune with their own values and institutions, much as they develop legal principles and procedures that are suitable to their social and cultural values and institutional practices. As a matter of principle, then, conflict management should be an appropriate subject of cross-cultural dynamics, one presumably marked by principles and practices some of which are universally valid, others particular to the given context. Such a cross-cultural approach could potentially be both enriching to the theory and practice of conflict resolution and effective in addressing context-specific problems.

Conclusion

The three areas of activity I have outlined in this paper are closely interconnected. The main issues concern the evolution of the

Sudanese identities that are now in conflict, the extent to which the symbols that divide those identities are more fictitious than real, and the prospects for uncovering the obscured realities and utilizing them in the process of nation building. To expose those realities and foster the desired unity requires education in the broad sense, part of which can be accomplished with relative speed but much of which will require time. My politically and culturally inspired novels are intended as contributions to this process. More practical efforts, however, are needed to help the Sudanese end the devastating civil war, which is clearly an unbearable burden on the country in both material and human terms. The personal initiative that General Obasanjo and I undertook in 1987 is one such attempt. The exercise itself has been a learning process for us, and we hope for the leaders of the warring factions as well. The value of this experience cannot be gauged by its effect on the war, which still rages, but rather by what it has taught us about the role of the participant-observer, principles of third-party involvement, and the potential for a cross-cultural perspective on conflict resolution.

Commentary on the Papers of Abdullahi An-Na'im and Francis Deng, Followed by General Discussion

Commentary by Mohamed Omer Beshir

I would first like to say how pleased I am to listen to both Mr. Deng and Mr. An-Na'im. I do agree generally with what they have presented; my approach might be a bit different, but on the basics we are in full agreement.

Before starting I would like to say that I wish to comment as a Sudanese. Mr. Deng has presented a southern Sudanese point of view. Mr. An-Na'im has given us a Muslim's view. I present my commentary as a Sudanese. There are many people in the Sudan, like me, who perceive themselves and would like to be perceived as Sudanese. Even using the terms *northern* and *southern*—many of us are becoming a bit sensitive about this. There is today in the Sudan a growing perception of a Sudanese identity.

First, I would make a general comment about religion and conflict. Really we are talking about religion and conflict, not religion and integration. Throughout history religions have been sources of conflict; people have often fought one another in the name of religion. The history of the world is full of conflicts between religions, or even within religions between different interpretations. Religion has been and continues to be in our present situation, unfortunately, a source of conflict. We must take this into consideration first.

Second, to focus on our subject at hand, Mr. Deng has suggested the complexity of the cultural map of the Sudan. I would add that the *religious* map of the Sudan is much more complex than has been presented up to now. (I am not, of course, referring to what Mr. Deng has presented today.) In the Sudan, we categorize people as Muslims, Christians, and non-Muslims/non-Christians. But within these groups there are varieties and different subgroups. For example, within the Muslim group there are, as we know, religious sects or Sufi orders. These sects number up to thirty subgroups—thirty organizations within the Muslim group. From the Qadiriyya to the Khatmiyya to the Ansar to the Ahmadiyya to the Idrisiyya to the Sanusiyya, Tijaniyya . . . Within the Christian group we know very well that there are the Catholics, the Protestants, and other different subgroups that do not necessarily agree all of the time. Within the non-Muslim/non-Christian group we have of course different subgroups. So I would like to suggest that the Sudan has really a very complex religious map. We need to lay out that map clearly and present it to ourselves. In order to get out of the mess we are in, we must know what are the facts. We need to know how these groups and subgroups relate to each other.

Third, we speak of the multicultural south and the Arab Muslim north. I would say that the north is not so homogenous; there are exceptions. You have to remember the Nuba mountains. The people there are not Muslims. This is quite a large group. In southern Kordofan there are Christians. The southern Blue Nile has Muslims, but it has also got Christians. There are pockets of Christians to be found in the northern Sudan in such places as Atbara, Port Sudan, El Obeid. All the urban areas have Christian groups. In addition, the number of non-Muslims coming from the southern Sudan as a result of the war or as a result of the famine has increased. They have grown into very large and influential pockets in the northern Sudan. In the north we even have groups that were originally not Sudanese: the Copts from Egypt, the Armenians, the Greeks—all are now Sudanese Christians in the north. So we have this picture of a multicultural south and a homogenous north. But the number of non-Muslims in the north with different origins, different identifications, is increasing.

Commentary

Fourth, I would point out that the south cannot be characterized as simply Christian. The majority of the population is non-
Muslim/non-Christian. Seventy percent of the population of the
southern Sudan, if the population is four or five million, is non-
Muslim/non-Christian. They are a *very* large proportion of the
population. Christianity is only predominant among the elite.
You have a Christian elite, but not a Christian people. So in talking about the Sudan and the issue of national integration, one has
to take that very much into account.

There have been two phases of Christian penetration in the
Sudan. The first was pre-Islamic Christianity, which was a peaceful penetration. The second penetration was fostered by the first
colonial system, the Turco-Egyptian regime. We have to remember that it was a Turco-Egyptian Ottoman Islamic regime which
encouraged the Christian missionaries and helped them to pene-
trate and launch their missionary activity. The next phase of colonialism, the British system, discouraged the Christianization of
the north, encouraging missionary activity only in the south
under what we have come to know as the sphere system. However,
here I disagree with the argument that the British colonial system
was neutral toward or "lived with" Islam in northern Sudan. The
colonial attitude was more complex. The British colonial system
resisted Mahdism, fighting against it because Mahdism was perceived as the enemy. But it collaborated with another subgroup,
with the Khatmiyya and the other anti-Mahdist groups. So religion was used under the colonial system to manipulate the political structure of the Sudan during the Condominium.

One must note that as Christianity became involved in
Sudanese politics in the 1890s, so did Sudanese Islam. The
Mahdist movement was, I suggest, the first and most significant
anticolonial movement. Colonialism here, during the Mahdist
first phase, means *turkiyya*, the Turks. To Mahdists, the Ottomans
were as much infidels as the infidels themselves! Mahdism as a
religious sentiment and a political movement was a revolutionary,
national movement that played a significant role in the history
and development of Sudanese life. The Mahdist system had no

time to develop a state—only fifteen years. There was fighting all of the time. The Mahdist state was at best a perception of the Ansar at the time. I do not think we can assert more than this. Then we have to say also that the Ansar movement during the Condominium adapted the Mahdist tradition, and now the Umma party has been adapting the Mahdist perception to promote its vision of what the state should be like in the modern world. These were and are the inheritors of a tradition trying to work out what the Mahdi, the revolutionary, the anticolonialist, was trying to establish in the Sudan.

If we talk about the Mahdi, we should mention the rival Khatmiyya. With a foreign origin, the Khatmiyya became a collaborator and friend of the Turkish regime and its foreign system. Of course, one of the goals of Mahdism was to drive out not only the Turks, but also those who collaborated with the Turks. So the image of Mahdism is not only one of a Muslim group, but of an anticolonial group as well. Later both Mahdism and the Khatmiyya sided with the nationalists against the colonial regime, but I will not dwell on that except to say that one has to realize that the legitimacy of the Sudanese political system was preserved by the sectarian groups.

In the postindependence era, if we are going to talk about the present situation, about Islam, about religion, we have to talk about the present war. I would like to suggest that it is no longer a north-south war; anyone trying to argue that it is a north-south war does not know what is going on. This is a civil war. The opposition is not composed only of southerners. Their leadership is not only southern, and not only Christian; nor is it only an elite. So one cannot speak of the present conflict in terms of north and south.

As Mr. An-Na'im has been saying, the *immediate* cause of the war rests in the September laws [imposition of Sharia]. The people who oppose them are not necessarily southerners: there are Muslims in the north who are against the September laws. So it is not true to say that the northerners accept these laws. I would like to say that there is no direct correspondence between acceptance or rejection of the Sharia laws and being a Muslim or being a non-Muslim. There are may good Muslims who say, "I am a Muslim but I am against the September laws," either for the reasons Mr. An-Na'im has laid out or because the laws violate the constitution and human rights—both of which the government is formally committed to upholding.

The laws discriminate between Sudanese, but in building a nation you cannot have a majority and a minority. Both Mr. An-Na'im and Mr. Deng have referred to a growing perception of *this* democratic system. Is it legitimate to talk about majorities and minorities within a society like that of the Sudan, with one hundred languages and so many cultural divisions—not north and south, but a multiple and complex system?

Mr. Deng has referred to the fact that the elites of both the north and south are all products of a Western educational system. To me, although they have been exposed to the same system, they are all entrenched in their own local cultures. That is why, I think, one must say that in the Sudan there are no Arabs. At best there are only Arabized Sudanese. We have all these different degrees of Arabization, but no Arabs. Neither the elites nor the local people identify themselves as Arabs.

Mr. An-Na'im has provided one kind of answer to the question, Which Islam are we talking about? Islam of the Saudis? Islam of Iran? Islam of Egypt? Is it the Islam of [Dr. Hasan] Turabi? Is it the Islam of Nimeiri? If there is one thing we are all agreed on, it is that the Islam of Nimeiri is irrelevant. One thing the Sudan is agreed on is to get rid of the September laws. What we are not agreed on is how to go about it, how to keep the country together and preserve an identity that is Sudanese. So the challenge is really [to erase] the polarization around religion as it is interpreted by the Sudanese fundamentalists. Their interpretation is rejected by all Muslims; I do not know of any group except those who made the laws who accept them. So the interpretation is rejected by everybody, and today Mr. An-Na'im gave us an argument for rejecting the [September] laws that is nevertheless Islamic. It is an argument that needs to be understood generally.

Finally, I think the challenge today is to create a Sudanese state with a Sudanese system. A Sudanese Islam has worked very well for us. We need a Sudanese Islam as we need a Sudanese Christianity. We need a system on a new model that takes all of this into consideration. So the challenge is to create not a Muslim or a non-Muslim or an anti-Muslim state, but a state that is Sudanese.

Commentary by Ibrahim Abu-Lughod

On the one hand, I am conscious of the very specific issues that have been raised addressed specifically to the Sudan and therefore the insistence of Mr. Omer Beshir on a particular Sudanese solution or Sudanese conceptualization of the national problem. While I sympathize with that on a number of grounds, as I listened to Mr. Deng and then to Mr. An-Na'im I tried to define *myself.* Culturally I am an Arab. (I still do not know what this means.) Territorially I am Palestinian, much in the same way that all three of you [Mr. Deng, Mr. An-Na'im, Mr. Beshir] are Sudanese. (We do not know what that means exactly either.) Racially—that category does not exist in Palestine, although it has in the past—let us assume as a hypothesis (since we are all products of layers and layers of identities) that I am probably Canaanite. [Laughter] And I am probably Philistine! [Laughter] So as I reflect on the politics of Palestine, I reflect on them in the same way that I think my Sudanese colleagues reflect on the political problems of the Sudan.

We are after the creation of a state that would make it possible for culturally diverse people, whether in terms of perception or in terms of reality, [to coexist]. It doesn't make any difference if I only perceive myself as an Arab. I do not know what being an Arab means, but I do know that I can identify with all those who speak Arabic. I may be inspired [by them], I may be antagonistic to them, but it is a fact that when I am pressed against the wall to identify myself, I do. I say culturally I am an Arab; I can go all the way from Morocco to Yemen and feel that this is my national patrimony. But on a local scale I say I am part of this "Palestine," and

Palestine happens to be the center of very diverse, conflictual groups. So we also have a national war. And we are driving for a solution that would make it possible for people, irrespective of their loyalties, irrespective of their ethnicities, irrespective of their culture, irrespective of their specific identification in fact, to create a state that would make it possible for all of them to coexist in harmony, not in conflict, on the basis of equality.

Now, is this unique to either Palestine or the Sudan? This is actually where I prepared my comments. That is, I think the two papers are very thoughtful papers, and obviously I appreciate the particular thrust on the Sudan that is present here. I think that Mr. Deng tried to put the conflict in very objective, very analytical terms so that our emotions do not side with either north or south (historically, the north has oppressed the south) but also to discuss the role of history in the making of that conflict. So we have a problem, which Professor Beshir identified as a national problem. That is, I think, a correct designation. It is not a north-south, but a national question.

The national question is of two dimensions. One dimension is the intercommunal conflict between the north and the south, the different ethnicities. As Mr. Beshir said, there are many ethnicities, which have many different loyalties and commitments and so forth. There is also another conflict that resides essentially within the hegemonic group and that has an implication for the national question. Now, I think if we view the formation of the Sudan—I mean, even the term means simply the country of the blacks, that is all it means. Now, in the medieval Arabic literature with which I am familiar, the *Bilād al-sūdān*, as it is known, refers to *all* the countries of the blacks that now are territorially sovereign states. At present there is only one country that narrowly defines itself as "the Sudan." So the old Arab definition that included all of what was known as the "land of the blacks" is now in fact restricted to one country, the republic [of the Sudan]. Now, that has a very important implication. There is one thrust in Sudanese history that makes the identity of the Sudan, one that is essentially pre-colonial—that retains the old identity but gives a certain degree of authenticity to the present political entity. But the frontiers, as all of you know, are frontiers imposed by colonialism. They are not the frontiers of the Islamic state. They are not the frontiers of the Coptic state. They are not the frontiers of anybody! The frontiers that we know in African states, as well as in the Middle East states, as well as in Asia, are all colonial frontiers.

Now, the irony of "independence" is that we all fight to preserve those frontiers. We shed blood to keep them. I speak as an outsider to the Sudan, although I am related in identity, but it seems to me that there may be absolutely no reason whatsoever for the north and the south to fight. Perhaps they do not belong to each other. If we can go into the process of state formation, on the one side we are saying that the Sudan today is a product of these two historical thrusts: one is the Islamic, which is also a hegemonic group that came from the north, came from other areas and imposed a political, cultural, and religious system by coercion or by persuasion—it does not make any difference, the system is a reality; then you have a colonial enterprise that came and lumped pieces together, allowed certain things to take place in a particular area. I know we get sick and tired of hearing about the role of missionaries, but now I understand that even the Ottomans have contributed to the process of Christianizing the south. That may be true, but the Ottoman state also helped in Christianizing in Lebanon, in Syria, in Palestine, in Egypt, wherever the Ottomans ruled—not because they wanted to assist the process of Christianization, but because the Ottoman state was being coerced by imperialism, which was working to dismantle it. I think it very important for us to remember those forces that went into the creation of the present entity.

Now, the issue of the hegemonic group in present-day politics, I think, is important. That is, there is a very serious conflict within the hegemonic group. That conflict could be partly ideological, or it could be using ideology as a cover—that is, we use Islam as a cover for other issues over which we fight. Let me suggest to you that most human history is a conflict over interests, over making a living, over property, over the material things and not over spiritual things. I think the spirit is a cover for the materialist conflict, and therefore within the hegemonic group I think there is a serious class interest. Between the hegemonic group—that is, the Arab Islamic north—and the other parts of the Sudan, I think, there is a conflict of communities. Here I want to call attention to the importance of comparative studies in understanding the specific thrusts in the Sudan's question. We have a total disintegration of the state in Lebanon, which is not Islamic, where the hegemonic group was not Islamic but Christian. The war that was fought in Lebanon was between "Christians" and "Muslims," but at least those of us who accept the materialist interpretation of history know that in actuality there was a tremendous amount of class conflict in Lebanon in which the Muslim elite and the Christian elite collaborated against their own constituents. I suggest that if we allow ourselves to use empirical studies in the case of the Sudan, to just look into the possible variables which are essentially social and economic, perhaps the religious dimension of the conflict will turn out to be not as significant as we depicted either between the north and the south or within the north itself.

I think there are important distinctions which have been introduced by Mr. An-Na'im. I found very intriguing the distinction between Islam and Sharia. I think this is an important distinction. I wonder if we can make it operational in the systems that are evolving both in the Islamic world at large and in the African world that is Islamic. I think if we study European history and the problem of European integration and state consolidation, there are certain facts that are known. We call Europe secular. Mr. An-Na'im tried to associate it with Christianity, but I do not think it is. The original distinction between that which is Caesar's and that which is God's I think may also be an ideological cover. I think there are objective forces in European history that went into transforming a Christian environment, giving rise to a Christian secular response. In today's America for example, a predominantly Christian country, there is a certain form of secularism that is peculiarly American. Now, that is not the same secularism as we have in Britain where the queen is the head of the church. Likewise when Makarios was the head of state in Cyprus, nobody said that this was a Christian state. But when a Muslim *shaykh* becomes the head of a state . . . My God! That is fundamentalism!

Well, I think we need to understand that each cultural community—the Jews, the Christians, and the Muslims—will give rise to a different kind of secularism, and the kind is specific to the culture. Here I want to fault our contemporary Muslims (and I am one of them) when we think of a secular political order where we have equal rights. I want to suggest that in fact the Ottoman state that we dismantled was much more advanced than the Islamic states of today. The first constitution that was promulgated in the Ottoman state was in 1876, and the first departure from Islamic tradition preferred the Islamic but gave equal rights. Non-Muslims were no longer *dhimmīs. Dhimmīs* became Ottoman citizens without transforming the Qur'an or the Sharia. In fact, the Ottoman constitution gave citizenship to Christians and Jews. It gave popular sovereignty, that is, the right of the citizen to participate in the political process—it assured it in the constitution. That is when we began to have elections. Without departing, without saying this was anti-Islamic or that it was transforming the Sharia; it began a process of change, gradually. In contrast, our current models, as Mr. Beshir said earlier, are inadequate, although they may prove useful for the moment. Egypt has gone very far on the path of secularism. It is not the same as Italy, but Italy is a secular state. Poland is a secular state, but we always talk about the power of the church. My suggestion is that in the Sudan I think the challenge, just as it is for the Palestinians whether they are Arab or Jews, is to find a political model that makes it possible for different communities to coexist, and clearly here the Western experience is very useful for state consolidation and so forth. That is, if we vest rights in the individual rather than in the community, we begin the process or we resume the process of state consolidation on terms to which we give rise and not on terms inherited from either the colonial European state or the Islamic state.

Discussion

MR. GAMBARI: I would follow Mr. Abu-Lughod in trying to present a comparative dimension to this morning's discussion of the Sudan. I have had the good fortune of having listened to both Mr. Deng and Mr. An-Na'im many times and in different fora. The more I listen to them the more I have two feelings: one is that I wish the kind of conversation they are having would be taking place in Africa rather than here because I think operationally they would have even more significance. Secondly, I find that as I listen to them, the differences, or what you perceive as the differences, between their positions seem to be narrowing, which I think is also positive for the prospect of national integration in the Sudan.

But as I said at the beginning, I am interested in a comparative dimension of this morning's discussion. I want to look at the situation in the Sudan and Nigeria, which is the country from which I come. I find that, as Mr. An-Na'im said, there are quite a number of parallels. First, there are no national political parties in either the Sudan or Nigeria (although efforts have been made to establish them in Nigeria—ethnicity being the major obstacle). Also, the Sharia issue in both the Sudan and Nigeria tends to be a very divisive issue—extremely divisive. And thirdly in terms of similarity, of course, we have the civil war, which has taken place and ended in Nigeria but has been taking place and continues in the Sudan.

However, I think that is where the similarity seems to end. Because I find that the immediate difference between the Sudan and Nigeria is the fact that national power as vested in the central government in Nigeria is far more diffuse both in theory and in practice. The theory of federalism and the application of a federal character in sharing important national positions, political offices as well as even in the bureaucracy, tends to be fully accepted in Nigeria (with *some* grudges here and there). Also the concept of regionalism, regional autonomy, and, now, states rights tends to be fully established in Nigeria. Moreover, in practice you find that if you look at the three indices of power in the case of Nigeria—economic power, political power, and bureaucratic power—you find that this has also been diffuse, with the southern ethnic groups dominating the economic and bureaucratic dimension of the state and political power almost invariably being held, at least at the topmost levels, by people from the north. So a big difference, I think, between Nigeria and the Sudan is that the concept of one majority tribe or a majority religion and therefore a hegemonic group is not nationally accepted in Nigeria. In fact, perhaps the difficulty in organizing an acceptable national population census in Nigeria relates to the fact that—not that we cannot count, I think we can count very well—sometimes we do not even want to know who is ahead in terms of religion or in terms of ethnic groups.

In fact, I would go on to argue that the opportunity for one major tribe or ethnic group to consolidate itself as a major force using religion to reinforce it may have been somehow possible in the late 1950s and early 1960s, particularly in northern Nigeria where real efforts were made by the then premier of the Northern Region, the late Sardauna of Sokoto [Sir Ahmadu Bello]. But that opportunity was lost, possibly never to be regained, because the first military coups of January and July 1966 and the civil war that followed in Nigeria led to the creation of states—from the original three, later four, regions to twelve states, then nineteen, and now twenty-one states. The idea of the secular state has now been entrenched in the constitution, in both the constitution of the First Republic and the Second. Even when the opportunity existed to create a dominant ethnic group or dominant religion in the north of Nigeria, the policy of a united north and the dominance of Islamic religion there was pursued imperfectly. I would argue it was mostly a defensive mechanism by the dominant group there in the north, the dominant religion of Islam there, against perceived domination of the north by the peoples of the south and by the religions of the south.

Discussion

I would say that in Nigeria we made a historic compromise that has two dimensions, one unwritten, one written, both of them very tentative and uneasy. The unwritten one is that the north will continue to provide the political leadership in Nigeria while the south will continue to somehow dominate the economy and the bureaucracy. This arrangement, of course, is not perfect. It has been challenged both in the north by Islamic fundamentalism and in the south because they feel that they are more advanced socioeconomically so why should they be subject to northern political domination. But that is the unwritten compromise. The written one is the federal constitution stating that Nigeria should be governed as a federal republic with power decentralized and a high level of local and regional autonomy. Also, religion was deliberately subordinated to other forces in relation to national integration.

So listening to the discussion on the Sudan and trying to provide this comparative dimension I ask myself: Why is it that the kind of historic compromises that were made in Nigeria and the concepts of federalism and regional autonomy remain such divisive concepts in the Sudan—almost as much as the idea of the secular state? Then I ask a leading question. In the state of the Sudan, what would result if they were to accept federalism, regional autonomy, and secularity? I am impressed that Mr. Beshir's comments seem to be treading along that path, that yes, the state of the Sudan is worth preserving even if you have to make compromises in terms of federalism and secularity. But then I ask myself, I wonder how much support does the kind of reasonableness heard this morning from Mr. Deng and from Mr. An-Na'im have in the Sudan itself in terms of the preservation of the Sudan as we know it today.

MR. AN-NA'IM: The historical compromise that you refer to is actually one of my points. It has always been the case in the Sudan, but it is only recently that it has been threatened. I have emphasized the spirit of cooperation and tolerance that existed and characterized northern Sudanese Islam throughout. It is only recently that this has been challenged, only since 1983 with the introduction of Sharia, which is the point I tried to emphasize.

In respect to the experience of the Ottoman Empire, Mr. Abu-Lughod pointed out that the Ottomans had achieved equality for non-Muslim citizens and allowed them to participate in affairs of the state without changing the Sharia. What they did actually was to displace Sharia: they did not reform Sharia itself. Under the pressure of European powers they only suspended certain aspects of Sharia. So these were not reforms in Sharia itself but only displacements of Sharia. This has characterized not only the Ottoman Empire, but also the Indian Mughal Empire and the Persian Empire. All of these Muslim empires capitulated to European powers by suspending certain aspects of Sharia, public aspects of Sharia, in order to gain certain advantages or certain benefits of membership in the international community.

The problem is that in all of these regions there is a reassertion of Sharia, because it was not reformed but only displaced. Now if the so-called fundamentalist Muslims succeed in trying to reintroduce Sharia, we will be taken back to what had been the case several centuries ago. That is why it is my position that we would not only suspend the application of Sharia but reform Sharia from an Islamic perspective so that when Islamic law is applied it would be acceptable. Actually, the experience of Iran is most significant here because as you know the shah and his father had gone very far in terms of secularization and westernization, but everything has been negated by Khomeini because the process of secularization and modernization was not seen as legitimate in Islamic terms, was only seen as a Western innovation introduced by the shah against the wishes of the people. Therefore it was easily replaced with Sharia by Khomeini.

Mr. Abu-Lughod said that Makarios was a head of the state in Cyprus but that we did not say Cyprus was a religious state;

when the queen of England is the head of state we do not say that it is a religious state. Of course, it is not that simple. You see, it is a question of the law that is enforced and the rights of citizenship. Regardless of the religion of the head of the state or even the formal subscription of the state, the question is the constitutional status and the rights of citizens. Because in Khomeini's Iran non-Muslims are disqualified by the terms of the constitution itself from holding office or participating in the political processes, Iran is a religious, theocratic state. But in Britain, Cyprus, or anywhere where the rights of citizens are not affected by their religion, it makes no difference who is the head of the state so long as that in itself is not an aspect of discrimination along the lines of religion. The point is, we have to look further than just the formal aspect of who is the head of state.

Both Mr. Abu-Lughod and Mr. Beshir made the point that religion is maybe a cover for other conflicts. I think that is true to some extent, but also I think it is in its own right a cause of conflict. The point is that to the extent religion is a cover to other conflicts, it has to be addressed even as a cover. So we cannot say that because it is a cover to socioeconomic conflicts we can simply disregard it. We have to deal with it even at that level. Secondly, religion is not the only cause of conflicts. We know that we have other causes of conflicts: even in societies that claim to be areligious, still there is conflict. So to the extent that religion is the cause or the cover of conflict, we have to deal with those aspects of it.

In regard to the multiplicity of identities within the country and the fact that the northern Sudanese are not Muslims in a monolithic sense, and neither are the southern or non-Muslim Sudanese, of course that is true. I would like to suggest that in fact cultural diversity and cultural conflict are healthy and desirable. The only issue is how they are resolved or readjusted or negotiated. So long as cultural competitions are resolved in a constitutional, orderly framework that allows for equality of opportunity to compete and to express and so on, I think that is very fine and healthy and must be preserved. However, when you have a situation where the majority or dominant group is not only insisting on asserting its identity but imposing it on others by force, that is where you have very serious conflict. As a Muslim myself, I do believe that Muslim Sudanese should continue to have their Islamic identity, whatever variety it may be, so long as the rights of non-Muslim Sudanese as citizens of their state are not in any way adversely affected.

The final point: I do not believe the claims of the current government that they are going to achieve equality for non-Muslim Sudanese while maintaining or introducing alternative Islamic laws. Someone suggested to me that as long as the result would be good, revising Sharia should not be objectionable even if the regime is not saying openly that it is revising Sharia. Why should I bother and insist that we must be clear about this? My reason for objection is that I do not believe them. Realistically speaking, I do not believe that they will in fact achieve equality for non-Muslims. What I am saying is that these arguments are political ploys to defuse the conflict in the south, to disarm opponents of Sharia for the time being. But when it comes then to implementation, Sharia is not going to be implemented by the heads of state personally, it is going to be implemented by the judges, by juries, by other *fuqahā'* and *'ulamā*. I would also note the prevailing view in the country at large. Unless these leaders are willing to say, "Look, this is going to be the law: one, two, three, four," explicitly stating in what ways Sharia is going to be changed, when it comes to practical implementation the law that will be implemented in day-to-day practice will be Sharia because that has not been changed authoritatively. In that situation we will have lost the goodwill once again of non-Muslim Sudanese and it will be extremely difficult to achieve certain terms for national reconciliation.

MR. GAMBARI: What I am asking is—this question of historic compromise is very important in my view—Why is it that the Sudan cannot be declared a "Federal Republic of the Sudan" and a secular state where power in the center can be shared, not dominated by any ethnic group, but sharing power at the center? I do not see that that has been made clear. Why not a true federal republic with power being shared at the center, not dominated by any one group and so elastic as to be not only written into the constitution but practicalized.

MR. AN-NA'IM: Of course, I welcome achieving the benefits of secularism that may be brought about by a federal arrangement, but the problem is that for Muslims the Qur'an is very explicit: those who do not rule according to Islam are unbelievers and the wrongdoers and so on. This makes it difficult for Muslims to implement an explicitly secular state, and actually the reverse of the secular state in predominantly Muslim countries like Iran and Pakistan and so on testifies to this fact. Now, the question is whether we can achieve the benefits of secularism *through* an Islamic argument. This is my position. I have not explained it in detail here because I do not believe it is the subject of the debate here. If you can achieve complete equality for Muslims and non-Muslims, women and men, and remove every feature of discrimination in terms of public law or criminal law or every other aspect, then what you have from a Muslim perspective is an effectively secular state with Islamic justification or orientation, and from a non-Muslim perspective a secular state, because as far as a non-Muslim is concerned the Islamic argument is irrelevant. Now, the question is whether we can do that, a question of reinterpretation to achieve it.

MR. LAITIN: I think Mr. Gambari's is the relevant question to ask, a crucially important one requiring further discussion. As I see it, Mr. Gambari's analysis is that the historic compromise came from the different sides of the conflict, say in the Nigerian civil war from the east and the north, as it were, recognizing that this thing could not go on anymore and that something else was needed. Why cannot the Sudanese get a historic compromise of this sort?

The conventional wisdom in the Nigerian case, however, suggests there was a social basis for the historical compromise, and the social basis for that compromise was in the fact of the minorities. The minorities in Nigeria were well situated in the bureaucracy, well situated in the economy, and they were the ones who were interested in Nigeria, including the general [Yakubu Gowon] who led the war from the north. The people who made up the minorities felt that the Biafran state would be a tremendous threat to the minorities in the east and that a northern state would be a tremendous threat to the people of the Middle Belt. So you had very large significant groups in Nigeria—up to 50 percent of the population—who had an interest in Nigeria and a strong interest against the three regions having autonomy. The fact that you had well situated and polit- ically powerful groups that had penetrated the bureaucracy and the economy who had an interest in Nigeria made a tremendous change in the civil war attitude. I remember read- ing in 1966 that one of the northern leaders had said, "Well, let those *****s go! Who cares?" The answer was that there *were* people who cared, including Gowon himself, who is a Middle Belt Christian from the north.

The question then arises: If the conventional wisdom is cor- rect about Nigeria, about the social basis of the minorities hav- ing the interest in pushing this historic compromise, what is the situation in the Sudan? Is it comparable? Well, we have heard some data from the three speakers agreeing that the mosaic in the Sudan is complex—that is, numbers of leading Muslims in the south, numbers of Christians in the north, cross-cutting cleavages from north and south, with Mr. Beshir being the most explicit on this, but the other speakers mentioning it. My sense is, and this is based on what they said and not from any inde- pendent knowledge of the Sudan, that the social basis of minorities in the Sudan is much weaker than the social basis of minorities in Nigeria. To merely ask for sensitive northerners sensitive to the interests of the south, or sensitive southerners sensitive the the interests of the north, as were our two main speakers—to ask them to make that compromise, I think, is socially, historically, unrealistic. However good-willed they are, they have to keep a bargaining position with their own con- stituencies, which if they were actually in their country would be pushed to more radical positions—as the leadership of the north and south has been in the last ten or fifteen years. So the real question is not how to make the leadership of the south or the leadership of the north more sensitive to each other, but how to promote or how to get a voice for those minority interests which I believe are the source of historic compromise in Nigeria.

MR. DENG: I would like to underscore what Mr. Abu-Lughod said about there being other material areas of conflict which are being in a sense camouflaged by the religious differences. That is absolutely true. If there were no consequences to being a Muslim, a Christian, a pagan, or what-have-you, the problem would not be as acute as it is. Where it comes into the picture is that these identificational labels become in a sense your card, your credit card for enjoying those material benefits. Therefore, we cannot sidestep these identificational symbols, even though you are absolutely right that they become a means of unfairly distributing or unevenly distributing the other resources, power, and material advantages involved.

Now, regarding my good friend Mr. An-Na'im. I had started by saying that we had areas of differences, and I thought Mr. Gambari was absolutely correct in pointing out that they seem to be diminishing. . . until Mr. An-Na'im made his explanation, when they came back again! [Laughter] The area of difference is this: as a non-Muslim, if I am to accept that we change the attitude of the majority who are Muslims, I have to get into the interpretation of their religion in order to bring out the most liberal aspect that would then make me equal. Right there I have been subordinated. It makes it very difficult. I mean, as noble as the idea is that I entirely agree with the end result, it really means that I have to accept a framework which is Islamic, from which I would then be liberated to be equal to the Muslims.

What Mr. Gambari is saying is we should remove religion and say that any subjection of the state to any particular religion divides. I am saying that the traditional religions of Africa have a lot in common with Islam in making religion become the basis for everything. The only difference is, as I have said, in the traditional African system there is an autonomous approach to religion, which means you have your clan divinities, your ancestors, and other intermediaries before you get to God, which essentially makes religion a personal matter. Whereas in Islam there is not that devolution of religious authority or that autonomous approach to religion. I would therefore say that despite the liberalism of Mr. An-Na'im, because of these different approaches to God, even a reformed Sharia would still subordinate non-Muslims to the generous interpretations of the Muslims.

Mr. Beshir made some very good remarks from the perspective of the Sudanese. My only quarrel with him—and I entirely agree with everything he said, but I do have a quarrel with him, and that is to label us as representing the north and south and *himself* as representing the Sudan. [Laughter] We all try to represent the Sudan, but we still get labeled. He too gets labeled, I am sure, by others who will think that he must be saying something that is northern. What I want to say is that to a very large extent we cannot avoid our labels. We do our best to transcend them, but we are still labeled.

Now, I really believe that there is sufficient basis in the history of the Sudan, in the thinking of today, and in the liberal element that Mr. Beshir was referring to, for a possible approach to a uniting vision of the Sudan. But that requires leadership. The problem with our leadership today is that it tends to reflect the divisiveness and the factionalism of the situation, maybe because through democracy they must return to a people who really have not been educated enough to see their vision for the nation. There are people who automatically adhere to their religious leaders and all that. The question, therefore, is where do we get that kind of leadership that will genuinely be uniting? Sometimes we tend to think of the military as the easy way out, but that, too, has its own problems and fundamental negation of other important values like democracy. The question is, Where is the leadership? I would agree with Mr. An-Na'im here—because of that religious tradition in Islam there is lack of moral courage for Muslim liberals to rise up and speak loud as to what must be done to unify the country. They tend to talk behind the scenes or be clever in manipulating religious concepts in order to open up, but no leader comes out with the clear moral courage to speak out.

MR. HAMDANI: The situation in the Sudan is very complicated because various historical processes have made it so—the process of islamization, et cetera. I think Mr. Gambari's comment is important: that a federal approach can be useful in creating a sense of unity. Also Mr. Beshir's comment that a "Sudan" consciousness, as opposed to other things, will also bring about that unity is important.

Mr. Laitin has analyzed what is the basis of the difference between the Sudan and Nigeria in terms of the status of minorities. Apart from that, two solutions come to me from what I have heard just now. One is the adoption of not only a federal, but a *con*federal approach, with a maximum of autonomy for the various parts of the land, if one wants to preserve the unity. The maximum autonomy comes from a confederal rather than a federal concept. Secondly, religion is important for all groups involved. An approach must be taken in such a way that the present world tendency of pursuing fundamentalism is turned into pursuit of a *liberal* fundamentalism (as there was once upon a time). Not fundamentalism that goes back to the retrogressive practices of the past, but goes back even further to a certain spirit of the religion, which was the spirit of reform and the spirit of change. With that sort of respecting and liberal fundamentalism, which was used, as has been suggested, by the Ottomans in granting citizenship, it was used in Tunisia, it was used effectively in many places—if this is done, combine a confederal republic and a new approach to religion, then one would not have to work to define the state as an Islamic state, an Arab state, a secular state—just a state with every part of it coexisting.

MR. DENG: The important point I wanted to make has to do with the admirable vision of Mr. Beshir that the war has become a civil war and that we have transcended the south-north barriers. I would like to say that whereas this is an admirable vision, the reality is still that by and large factions are drawn along those lines, even if we would like to transcend them. The movement does claim to represent the nation as a whole, but when we have met, as we did recently in Harare, where we organized a meeting to which delegates came representing the nation as a whole, it was seen as an optimistic step toward national unity, but something of a joke.

MR. HUNWICK: I am reminded of a character who used to appear on the BBC radio "Brains Trust" many years ago, Professor C.M. Joad. Whenever he was asked a question about anything he always started off, "Well . . . it all depends what you mean by . . ." [Laughter] I think that here it all depends on what you mean by "religion," and certainly it all depends on what you mean by "Sharia." I think I shall have to come back to those questions this afternoon.

The Role of Religion in National Life: Reflections on Recent Experiences in Nigeria IBRAHIM GAMBARI

Introduction

In today's Nigeria, various Christian denominations ranging from Anglican to Roman Catholic, Methodist, Baptist, Seventh Day Adventist and many others coexist peacefully with each other and with the Islamic faith as well as with traditional religions.[1]

This official, almost idealistic, view of the relationship within and between the various religious faiths in Nigeria contrasts sharply with the more recent reality of religious tensions and riots in the country. Indeed, the frequency and destructiveness of intra- and interreligious riots have undermined domestic peace and threatened political stability in Nigeria, particularly in the 1980s.

This paper will examine the recent crisis dimensions of the relationship between the major Nigerian religions, in contrast to the relatively high degree of religious tolerance in Nigeria from the decade of independence to the mid-1970s. Crises have ways of sharpening issues, highlighting remote and immediate causes of conflicts and the manner and types of arrangements made for resolving them.[2] Therefore, a closer look will be taken here at the controversy generated by the debate over Sharia in the Constituent Assembly which preceded the Second Republic; the religious riots in Kano (December 1980), Maiduguri (1982), Yola (1984), Gombe (1985), and the most recent one in Kaduna State (March 1987); as well as the sharp national division over the membership of Nigeria in the Organization of Islamic Conference (OIC) in 1986. These crises of religious intolerance call for some general reflections on the role of religion in the national life of Nigeria and some conclusions on the way forward.

It is necessary at this point to give some background and historical dimension to the issue of religious interaction in Nigeria. Of the two major nontraditional religions that came to what is presently Nigeria, Islam and Christianity, Islam made the earliest external contact, perhaps as early as the ninth century, through North Africa, Kanem-Borno, and later the Hausa states. The religion brought a new system of ideas, a new way of life, and literacy, by means of the Arabic and ajami scripts. Initially confined to a very small segment of the aristocracy and courtiers of some Hausa rulers, the religion expanded rapidly after the early-nineteenth-century jihad led by Shehu Usman Dan Fodio. Sokoto, the city of the Shehu, became the religious and administrative capital of the theocracy of the Fulani Empire, which would eventually cover most of the modern region of northern Nigeria. The Islamic faith later spread to the south of Nigeria, particularly parts of Yorubaland or the old Western Region of Nigeria.

Christianity, in contrast, came to Nigeria through the south. Originally brought by Catholic missionaries in the early sixteenth century, the religion was spread by Protestant missionaries much more widely from the middle of the last century as contact between the Europeans and the coastal and southern peoples of Nigeria increased. It was a religion associated with the coming of the Europeans first as explorers, then as traders, later as missionaries, and finally as colonial rulers. The westernization of Nigerian Christians was therefore inevitable and almost always welcomed by the old converted or new adherents.

Islam is now thought to be the most widespread of the religious faiths in the country, claiming adherents among perhaps 50 percent of Nigeria's population. In terms of geography, Islam accounts for about 70 percent of the population of the old Northern Region and about 20 to 30 percent of the population of the southern regions. It is important to note that Nigeria contains one of the largest Muslim populations outside the Middle East, which explains the interest that Saudi Arabia, Kuwait, Iran, Egypt, and some other countries of the Islamic world have shown toward Nigeria and Muslims there. While Christianity probably has fewer adherents than Islam relative to Nigeria's total population, it is the dominant religion in the southern regions of the country, and there are also very strong Christian minorities in the northern part of Nigeria. In addition, a large segment of the country's population follows neither of these two world religions of foreign origin; these people are sometimes referred to as animists, pagans, or followers of traditional religions.

The religious divide of Nigeria, then, is unbalanced regionally. That imperfect cleavage also extends to the ethnic divisions of Nigeria. Although most Hausa-Fulani and Kanuri peoples are Muslims, some Hausa-Fulani and minority ethnic groups in the northern part of Nigeria are strong Christians. The Yoruba people of western Nigeria, moreover, are split almost fifty-fifty between Christianity and Islam—an essentially equal division that makes Yorubas generally less extreme on religious issues in Nigeria.[3] Conversely, perhaps the minority status of Christians in the north is what makes them embrace their faith with such fervor. We shall return to these observations later.

The imperfections of the religious division in Nigeria affect the relationship between religion and other powerful factors in the political life of the country as well, principally ethnicity, regionalism, and growing class antagonism. Competition for political power in Nigeria has taken place largely within the framework of ethnic and regional divisions; certainly this was so in the period from the country's independence in 1960 to the first military coup in 1966.[4] The almost fourteen years of centralized and hierarchical military rule after the demise of the First Republic put something of an artificial lid on ethnic antagonisms. With the return to constitutional rule in 1979, serious attempts were made to reorient the competition for political power toward a national rather than an ethnic perspective. The constitutional provisions for the organization of political parties and the process for electing the president, as well as the electoral victory of the National party of Nigeria in the 1979 federal elections, pointed to a new weaker role for ethnicity in Nigerian politics. Unfortunately, because the politicians of the Second Republic did not try hard enough, they did not remain in power long enough to sustain the hopes generated for a new political order in Nigeria.

Religion neither displaced nor replaced ethnicity as the driving force of Nigeria's politics; it merely reinforced elements of ethnic antagonisms in the country. The role of religion as a reinforcer of ethnic conflict in Nigeria had much to do with the westernization that Christianity brought to the south, which included education, literacy, and access to jobs in the colonial service. The leaders of the largely Muslim north feared the prospect of domination by Christians from the south, especially after the country's independence. This fear may have informed the "northernization policy" of the Northern Region government, adopted to promote local talents and install them in administrative positions so as to check or eliminate the perceived southern domination of the regional civil service. Later, too, northerners demanded that the distribution of jobs at the center should be done in a way that reflected the "federal character" of Nigeria. At the same time, however, the peoples of southern Nigeria "feared that the Muslims would form a demographic majority which would permit the (Muslim, 'conservative') northerners to rule over the (Christian, 'progressive') southerners."[5]

The Major Crises of Religion and the State, 1979–87

In preparation for the return to constitutional rule, the Obasanjo military administration established a Constituent Assembly (with members partly elected, partly nominated) to debate the draft constitution for Nigeria's Second Republic. The draft constitution was submitted to the Constituent Assembly by a Constitution Drafting Committee made up largely of legal experts. Of the issues that generated the greatest heat, but eventually little light, the Sharia laws and legal system must be placed at the top. The protagonists (largely Muslim members of the assembly) argued that a Federal Sharia Court of Appeal should be established as an intermediary between the states' Sharia courts and the Supreme Court of Nigeria, their reason being that the Sharia courts are the principal avenues for justice in the Islamic world and the symbol of political freedom for Muslims in Nigeria, who constitute over half of the total population. On the opposing side, many Christians viewed the issue of Sharia and the proposed court of appeal as symbols of potential Muslim domination in Nigeria.[6]

The issue illustrated open and hidden suspicions between Christian and Muslim elites. On the one hand, the Muslims saw no reason why Christians would deny those who wished to use the Sharia courts the right to do so. The rights of non-Muslims, or even Muslims who did not wish to have their case heard by the Sharia court, were not to be jeopardized; therefore, the Muslims felt that by opposing the federal appeal court proposal the Christian members of the Constituent Assembly were hoping to thwart the political aspirations of Muslims at the center. On the other hand, the Christians in the assembly who opposed the court saw Muslim proponents as "religious fanatics," neojihad advocates in disguise who, unless they were checked, would seek the expansion of Sharia law until it penetrated the whole ship of state.[7]

The rhetoric on both sides was strident. Behind-the-scenes intervention by the military administration and the hard work of "moderates" in the assembly were required before a compromise solution could be found for the crisis: namely, there would be no new Federal Sharia Court of Appeal, but in cases where further appeals had to be made from the states' Sharia courts, a special committee of the Supreme Court, made up of justices versed in Islamic law, would be empaneled to hear them. Of the major Nigerian ethnic groups, the Yorubas took the least extreme position on this explosive issue and were at the forefront in the search for an acceptable compromise.[8] A direct Christian-Muslim conflict would probably have the worst impact on the Yorubas, owing to their divided religious allegiance.

Generally speaking, one would expect the historic and contemporary conflicts of the various Nigerian Christian denominations to cause great strains within the Nigerian Christian community.

In fact, however, in recent times there have been far more serious splits within the ranks of the Muslims, despite the general cohesiveness of Islam as a religion in Nigeria. For example, in December 1980 the radical Maitatsine or Yan Tatsine sect organized systematic riots and killings of fellow Muslims outside the sect in Kano. Combined police and army operations were required to quell the disturbances caused by Maitatsine and his followers. Although Maitatsine was himself killed in the Kano clash, there were resurgences of his movement in Maiduguri (1981), Yola (February 1984), and Gombe (1985)—all cities in the north (a significant fact, as we shall see). The various commissions of inquiry established to examine the causes of the intrareligious conflicts reported, among other things, that the movement considered its duty to be to cleanse Islam within Nigeria from the corrupt state into which it had descended. Members recruited into the sect, moreover, fought with great fervor; with little hope for early economic recovery in Nigeria, general discontent, especially in urban areas, and a high annual urban growth rate (estimated at between 5 and 6 percent, with 30 percent of the total population already living in cities), the pool of the "wretched of the urban masses" will likely continue to increase and fill the ranks of new "Islamic fundamentalism" repeatedly. We shall return to the class dimension of the religious conflict in Nigeria later. Suffice it here to say that as long as the violence involved only Muslims against Muslims and the poor against the poor, most Christians, as well as the wealthy of all religions, paid little attention. The state could handle it. Only when the poor turned on the rich and the Muslims on the Christians did the problems escalate, for then the state security agencies found it difficult to cope.

Such a situation did occur in Kaduna State in March 1987, perhaps the worst interreligious conflict in the recent history of Nigeria. For almost one week, violent attacks were made against life and property, mosques and churches, throughout the state. Security agencies appeared helpless as houses, hotels, restaurants, and places of worship were burnt down by irate mobs and many people lost their lives. In Zaria alone, over forty churches were destroyed, especially in Wusasa (home to several Hausa

Christians) and Sabon-Gari (nonindigenes' quarter). The riots began in Kafanchan, a strong Christian-minority town in Kaduna, over a religious disputation involving a man recently converted from Islam to Christianity and Muslim students at a teachers college there; it soon spread until the whole state was engulfed in acts of physical destruction. Had the religious riot- ing spread to other parts of Nigeria—which fortunately it did not—the result would have been disastrous for the stability and survival of the country as a unit.

The political and socioeconomic dimensions of this crisis should not, however, be downplayed. President Ibrahim Babangida said, in a national broadcast during the unrest, that the events represented the "civilian equivalent of an attempted military coup d'état." If that is so, the "success" of such an uprising must be attributed to the general climate of economic discontent and political uncertainty. The surest way to prevent religious "fire next time" is to take a hard look at the socioeconomic discrepancies between the rich and poor, north and south, rural and urban areas, Muslims and Christians. These issues, never properly addressed by successive governments in Nigeria since independence, have assumed much more serious dimensions in the 1980s.

I have mentioned that the most serious religious agitation and most strident class-based social and religious antagonisms have occurred in the northern cities. This reality, or even tradition, of radical political movements with religious overtones in some urban centers in northern Nigeria, especially Kano, contradicts the British colonial authorities' idealistic portrayal of a conservative, orderly, and peaceful north. Even prior to colonial rule, a division existed between the *talakawa* (commoners) and the ruling elite in Hausaland. And grafted upon this indigenous social class formation was Islam, a force for solidarity among workers from divergent ethnic and rural backgrounds and a means of integrating them into the new urban environment in which they found themselves.

Paul Lubeck, in his excellent study of Islam and urban labor in northern Nigeria, has identified two major processes at play in the region: the transition to semi-industrial capitalism and the world historical revival of Islamic fundamentalism. From the end of the Nigerian civil war to the pinnacle of Nigeria's success as an exporter of crude oil and member of OPEC in the late 1970s, the forces propelling Nigeria toward semi-industrial capitalism were strong. As the economy grew, the city of Kano grew rapidly (both spatially and demographically) as migrants sought wage employment in the manufacturing and service industries.[9]

These two processes did not produce, but rather reinforced the class-based Muslim groups that had operated in Kano for a long time, notably the Tijaniyya brotherhood. Islam fulfilled the need among Muslim Hausa-speaking workers for a common or community identity, social ritual, and system of meaning that linked them to their rural and precapitalist origins.[10] They insisted on the right to observe the daily prayers in their places of work, attended Friday congregational prayers, and taught or were taught Qur'anic and Islamic studies. As a result, they felt spiritually superior and purer, despite their poverty—or perhaps because of it—than the wealthy and more powerful Muslim brothers, who appeared to have abandoned or suspended their faith and the moral obligations of wealth.[11]

Another process at work was the development of *talakawa* nationalism, sharpened not only by the tremendous growth in the city's population but also by the *talakawa* origins of the bourgeoisie and petty bourgeoisie (traders, craftsmen, salaried employees, and even some *'ulamā'*).[12] This *talakawa* nationalism, in Lubeck's view, became a more fully developed class system thanks to the growing impact of state demands for greater revenues from taxation, with a resulting higher sense of class deprivation, as well as the "surplus extraction by the local aristocracy or *sarauta*, the colonial and post-colonial state and merchant capital."[13] The access to state patronage and privileges enjoyed by the upper classes also increased the general social division and inequalities.

Still, *talakawa* nationalism, including its sharpened class dimension, and the opposing interests of the *sarauta* and bourgeoisie in Kano found political expression in their differing party affiliations during the First and Second Republics. The urban workers and petty bourgeoisie often allied with the Northern Elements Progressive Union and, later, the Peoples' Redemption party under the charismatic leadership of the late Aminu Kano and the former governor of Kano State Abubakar Rimi. Conversely, the rest of the bourgeoisie and the *sarauta* aligned themselves with the dominant political party in the Northern Region, the Northern Peoples' Congress and later the National party of Nigeria.

While the channeling of the energies of the industrial workers and urban wage earners of Kano toward political activities, the growing sense of class maturity over the years, and the strengthening of trade union organization may explain that group's lack of participation in the violent, spontaneous forms of class conflict that pervaded the Yan Tatsine insurrections of the 1980s, that is small comfort to the Nigerian state.[14] The greater reality is that, compared to the early 1970s, the power, awareness, and tactical sophistication of the urban working class have increased. Nonetheless, this enhanced capability to wage a class struggle at the workplace and beyond could go in either direction. It found secular expression in the early 1980s, when party politics provided the outlet. During military rule, with a ban on party politics in place, the energies of the working people may well go in the other direction, that of Islamic nationalism. Lubeck pointed out, rightly, that a "radical Islamic populist ideology exists and appears attractive to the impoverished urban masses of Muslim Northern Nigeria."[15]

As long as the Yan Tatsine uprisings reflect what Lubeck calls "a deep structural contradiction within Islamic Hausa society [rather than] an isolated incident by some fanatics," there is a real danger that Islamic populism and violent agitation against both secular and religious authorities may increase.[16] In addition, drought or near-drought conditions and serious downturns in the economy would drive more and more rural poor into northern cities, many seeking out meager livelihoods as Koranic students or *leburori* (daily paid workers)—promising targets for recruitment into Yan Tatsine–type uprisings.

It could also be argued that the atmosphere of interreligious harmony was seriously poisoned by the issue of Nigeria's membership in the Organization of Islamic Conference (OIC), making the religious riots of March 1987 a disaster waiting to happen. Despite a growing challenge by Islamic fundamentalists and neofundamentalists, the concept of Nigeria as a secular state appeared to enjoy wide popularity in the country. Yet in 1986, without fully examining the sensitivity of such a decision, the federal military government applied for Nigeria to join the OIC as a full member. The act was soon leaked to the foreign and domestic press, generating a controversy reminiscent of the Sharia debate in the Constituent Assembly in 1976. Extremists on both sides threatened to tear the country apart if Nigeria were finally to join or withdraw from the organization. The old fears and suspicions were replayed. Once again, however, a compromise was fashioned, with the government establishing a Religious Affairs Council to look into the consequences of Nigeria's membership in the organization. This move was, of course, like bolting the stable door after the horse had escaped. The real purpose of the council was probably to repair the damage done to interreligious harmony in the country. Half Muslim, half Christian in makeup, the council found it most difficult to convene a successful meeting. Yet now that the OIC issue has been put on the back burner and tempers have cooled somewhat, the council can perhaps meet and pursue its wider mandate in the interest of peace and stability in Nigeria.

The religious crisis in Nigeria has four major trends. First, the most violent intrareligious conflicts have been those involving one world religion, Islam, but the most threatening to the country as a whole have tended to be those involving the two world religions. Second, the followers of traditional religions in Nigeria appear to be the most peaceful group, largely because of their general illiteracy and lack of articulation. Third, the separation of state and religion is becoming thinner and thinner as the coercive instruments of the state have to battle an increasingly open challenge from religious extremists and the far more dangerous threat posed by Islamic fundamentalism. More words on this in the conclusion. Finally, suspicion and fear generate extreme rhetoric from the opposing religious camps and often mask intense ethnic, regional, and class competition for socioeconomic gains from the state. Invariably, however, compromises are arranged that simply postpone the fundamental issues to another round of conflict in the future. The state has survived both group antagonisms within and between the two major religions and challenges to its secular nature. For how long this will continue remains to be seen.

Some Concluding Observations

Several other issues concerning religion, politics, the state, and the economy need to be raised with the hope that intellectual and practical efforts will be made to provide solutions for them. First, is it possible to make distinctions between the religious and political culture of a people? Perhaps in a purely intellectual or analytical sense this could be done. Some Western scholars, such as Talcott Parsons, would argue—wrongly, in this author's view—that the absence of such a distinction in a given society is an indication of its primitive nature. In his study of Kano, John Paden, while he did not go as far as Parsons, attempted to disengage the political (modern) from the religious (ancient) culture; the effort, however, could not be sustained by his theories and evidence.[17] Changes in religious culture have often produced changes in the political culture of Kano. And as Paden pointed out, the community dimension in Kano's political culture has historically rested on the notion that the primary boundaries of communal loyalties are religious. It may also be the case, at least for Kano and other sociologically similar cities in the old north, that community crisis (especially interethnic conflicts) can best be resolved by authority figures with fused religious and political roles.

Second, what is the situation for the rest of Nigeria's big ethnic groups? According to David Laitin, identification with a world religion is politically irrelevant in Yorubaland despite the tradition-sanctioned chieftaincy influence, if not authority, in that subregion of Nigeria. On the contrary, it is ancestral city politics and not world religion that works as a "pattern of group activity and serves as the dominant symbolic framework in Yorubaland."[18] Hence, calculations based on religious adherence are considered fanatic, irrelevant, or otherwise out of the realm of (political) import. The same may hold true for Ibos, even though tradition-based chieftaincy authority has not been strong among this republican people of the old Eastern Region of Nigeria. With the Edos and their Oba of Benin, conversely, quite the opposite is the case.

This question, while important by itself, also relates to the issue of ethnicity and religion in Nigeria. If, as argued earlier, religion did not create the problems of ethnicity that so hinder national integration, it nonetheless reinforced ethnic antagonisms in Nigeria. And if such issues as Sharia law and Nigeria's membership in the OIC contributed to the polarization of north and south, religion only makes a bad interethnic situation worse with regard to national unity and integrity.

Third, the contemporary experience of Nigeria may well represent the turning on its head of Marx's dictum that "religion . . . is the opium of the people." Religious fanaticism may constitute an instrument for the oppressed and dispossessed class to challenge the status quo in other sectors of national life. The downturn in Nigeria's economy since 1981 and the hardships caused by homegrown or IMF/World Bank–induced austerity and so-called structural adjustment programs have been having serious socio-economic consequences. A wave of armed robberies especially in the urban areas manifests the growing antagonism toward the affluent. Class consciousness is being increasingly raised, particularly on the part of the have-nots. The army of unemployed primary and secondary school leavers is being joined by growing numbers of unemployed university graduates as well as graduates from polytechnic and teacher training colleges. With urbanization growing at an annual rate of 5 to 6 percent in a total population of over 100 million people, which in turn is increasing at the rate of 3.4 percent annually, with about 50 percent of that national population consisting of young people under sixteen years of age, a real time bomb may be ticking in Nigeria's cities.

Popular discontent and frustration with prevailing socioeconomic conditions could find easy channels for expression through religious outbursts and riots carefully guided by disgruntled politicians or opposition segments of the national elite. Significantly, most of the violent intra- and interreligious conflict in Nigeria has taken place in the northern part of the country, which is considered to be more economically backward than the south. The imbalance in the distribution of economic gains since the country's independence among the major regions of Nigeria is clearly in need of urgent correction.

Finally, the secular nature of the Nigerian state has acquired new and powerful enemies, who are working to undermine the delicate balance of forces on this issue. One might of course ask whether the secular state of Nigeria should be preserved at all costs; or is it so fragile that whenever fundamental Muslim interests are discussed nationally the controversies generated threaten the very fabric of the state?

In support of secularism in Nigeria, of course, we have seen the positive role the Yorubas have played in defusing religious issues at the national level—at least up until the controversy over OIC membership. The intelligentsia in the north and probably in the rest of the country—who, if a religious state were established, would probably be even more marginalized at the national political level than they presently are—also appear to be on the side of religious tolerance and state secularism, as do most civil servants at the state and federal levels.[19] The old Islamic brotherhoods in Kano and other urban centers in the north have facilitated rural-to-urban and interurban transethnic connections, which can be mobilized in support of religious tolerance in the state. With new efforts toward education at all levels (primary, secondary, postsecondary, and even adult classes), too, Nigerians could be shown the virtues of religious tolerance as a potential instrument for strengthening the moral fiber and unity of the country. These combined forces could, in short, help to sustain the secularity of the Nigerian state. Yet this task would be worthwhile only if it means the protection and advancement of the religious rights of all, majority and minority alike, rather than serving merely as a cloak to perpetuate socioeconomic educational and bureaucratic advantages enjoyed by some sections or classes in the country.

One last word. There is an interesting story of a meeting between the first president of Nigeria, Dr. Nnamdi Azikiwe, and the late premier of the Northern Region, Alhaji Ahmadu Bello, the sardauna of Sokoto. The meeting reportedly took place around the mid-1960s amid growing tensions between the coalition partners in the central government (the northern-based Northern Peoples Congress and the National Council of Nigerian Citizens [formerly National Council of Nigeria and the Cameroons], which started as a national party but later became an ethnic-dominated party) and in an environment of growing divergences between north and south and ethnic antagonism. Dr. Azikiwe is quoted as having told the premier, "Let us forget our differences." To which the sardauna replied, "No: let us understand our differences. . . . By understanding our differences we can build unity in Nigeria."[20] There is a moral there for the future of the country, especially in the areas of interfaith relations and the role of religion in national integration.

Notes

1 *Perspectives of Nigerian Culture* (Lagos: External Publicity Division, Federal Ministry of Information, 1985).

2 See Richard Neustadt, *Alliance Politics* (New York: Columbia University Press, 1970), for a theoretical framework of crisis in the international politics of two allied nations, which is of some relevance to relations between two major religions in the same country.

3 See David D. Laitin, *Hegemony and Culture: Politics and Religious Change Among the Yoruba* (Chicago: University of Chicago Press, 1986).

4 See several studies on postindependence political developments in Nigeria, notably James S. Coleman, *Nigeria: Background to Nationalism* (Berkeley: University of California Press, 1958); F. A. Schwarz, *Nigeria: The Tribes, the Nation, or the Race* (Cambridge, Mass.: M.I.T. Press, 1965); and S. K. Panter-Brick (ed.), *Nigerian Politics and Military Rule: Prelude to the Civil War* (London: Institute of Commonwealth Studies/Athlone Press, 1971).

5 See Laitin, *Hegemony and Culture*, 6.

6 Ibid.

7 Ibid.

8 Ibid.

9 Paul M. Lubeck, *Islam and Urban Labor in Northern Nigeria: The Making of a Muslim Working Class* (Cambridge: Cambridge University Press, 1986), 1.

10 Ibid., 147–48.

11 Ibid., 160.

12 Ibid., 37.

13 Ibid., 305.

14 Ibid., 308.

15 Ibid., 309.

16 Ibid.

17 John Pden, *Religion and Political Culture in Kano* (Berkeley and Los Angeles: University of California Press, 1973).

18 Laitin, *Hegemony and Culture*, 183.

19 In a strongly worded press release entitled "Violent Politics of Religion and the Survival of Nigeria," several university lecturers condemned the violence of the religious conflict and called on the federal government to reaffirm Nigeria's status as a secular state. They stressed that religion should be left to the choice of citizens and that the federal government should protect the fundamental human rights, security of life, and property of all citizens (Press release, Ahmadu Bello University, Zaria, mimeo, 13 March 1987).

20 See John Paden, *Ahmadu Bello, Sardauna of Sokoto: Values and Leadership in Nigeria* (London: Hodder & Stoughton, 1986), 3.

Muslim-Christian Conflict and Political Instability in Nigeria   DON OHADIKE

The unity of Nigeria is threatened by perennial religious disturbances. Both Muslims and Christians have threatened secession;
indeed, some have suggested that many countries be carved out of
the nation to avert what they genuinely regard as imminent
bloodshed, a cry heard loudly soon after the 1987 religious riots in
Kaduna State. Although Nigerians have been told that Islam and
Christianity are religions of peace and love, the available evidence
points to the contrary. A major problem is that Nigerians have
been burdened with two universalistic religions that do not mix
properly. Muslims are infidels and so are Christians, depending
on which side you are on. This is not just a twentieth-century
phenomenon, nor does it have anything to do with the recent
resurgence of Islamic and Christian fundamentalism. Religion is
simply an intolerant institution. It brooks neither opposition nor
constructive criticism.

Some observers attribute the current religious tension in Nigeria to religious intolerance and fanaticism; others, to the tendency
of many Nigerians to mix politics with religion; and still others,
to the manipulation by individuals of religion for personal
gain.[1] Although these factors certainly have contributed to the
religious crisis, they are not sufficient to explain the recent killings and burning and destruction of churches, mosques, homes,

This paper is a recasting of a presentation made at the First Annual Seminar
on Contemporary African Issues sponsored by the Program of African Studies
and the Committee on International Studies, Northwestern University,
Evanston, 28 May 1988.

automobiles, and business properties in certain parts of Nigeria. The 1987 upheavals in Kaduna State were unnecessary and could have been avoided. Yet the danger of another outbreak still looms, and it requires no gift of prophecy to predict that the country may not survive further widespread religious disturbances. The nation was fortunate that the 1987 riots were confined to Kaduna State alone. Had they spread into other states or into the armed forces (which are almost evenly divided between the two major religions), or had they occurred during a civilian regime, the story would have been too dreadful to recount.

This paper will identify some of the causes of the current Muslim-Christian tension in Nigeria and suggest how it might be halted for the sake of national survival and stability. We must begin by recognizing that Islam and Christianity were founded on two distinct and opposing religious ideologies, one based on the prophethood of Muhammad, the other on the divinity of Christ, and that the mere declaration that Nigeria is a secular state is not enough to bridge this ideological gulf. In fact, the very term *secular state* offends some people, for whom it is synonymous with an "irreligious society" or "Godless state." To build a truly multireligious nation, therefore, it is necessary to go beyond declarations and definitions and counteract those sentiments that breed religious arrogance and bigotry. Nigerians must decide whether they want a theocratic state or a modern nation-state, whether they prefer religious revivalism to scientific and technological advancement in a modern world, and, above all, whether they prefer several independent countries, some Islamic and others Christian, to one strong multireligious nation.

The Polarization of Nigeria Along Religious Lines

The current religious crisis in Nigeria derives from the country's religious polarization, which has strong historical roots. Islam was introduced into Nigeria in the eleventh century, and by the nineteenth century, it had become the religion of the Hausa, the Fulani, and the Kanuri. Starting from about 1804 the Fulani succeeded in extending Islam into the so-called pagan strongholds, as far south as the Niger River into Kwara and Afenmai.

As for Christianity, foreign missionaries began working in southern Nigeria in the mid–nineteenth century, but it was only after the effective establishment of British colonial rule in the twentieth century that the religion gained a real footing. From the coastal towns Christianity followed the new motor roads and railway lines into the interior. Although some missionaries had started to establish churches in northern Nigeria as early as 1909, they were strongly opposed by the Muslim emirs and British colonial officials. Thus, the missionaries contented themselves with evangelizing the non-Muslim communities in southern Zaria, Plateau, Benue, and Gongola.

After the British colonial adventurers overran the Sokoto caliphate between 1900 and 1903, Sir Frederick (later Lord) Lugard went about reorganizing the region under the indirect rule system. From northern Nigeria Muslim clerics, traders, and craftsmen carried Islam southward, using Ilorin as an important outpost for islamizing Yorubaland. At the same time, some Muslim ex-slaves from Brazil and Sierra Leone began to spread Islam in the Lagos area, to be joined in the 1920s by the Ahmadiyya missionaries from India.[2] Why these Muslims did not consider it necessary to work in southeastern Nigeria and the delta is still a puzzle; had they worked there as well as in western Nigeria, and had British officials allowed the Christian missionaries a free hand in the north as they allowed them in the south, certainly Nigeria would have developed into a healthy multireligious nation and its people been spared the present religious crisis.

Today the Yoruba are among the very few multireligious ethnic groups in Nigeria because both Islam and Christianity were allowed to spread freely among them. Indeed, the Yoruba have almost bridged the ideological gulf that separates the two religions, making it possible for individual members of households or extended families to practice both. As David Laitin has reminded us, the Yoruba have not politicized their religions;[3] their

moderate stand in heated national issues, like the Sharia debate of
1976–78, has thus helped to diffuse religious and political tensions
in the country. Furthermore, the Yoruba have benefited from the
innovations brought to Nigeria by Islam and Christianity. They
have produced more alhajis and imams than any other ethnic
group in southern Nigeria, and likewise more doctors, lawyers,
and accountants. The Yoruba, unlike most Hausa and Igbo,
would feel as at home in Mecca or Jeddah as they would in London or Washington. It is equally praiseworthy that the Yoruba
think of themselves first as Yoruba, rather than as Muslims or
Christians. For the sake of national stability, however, they should
be encouraged to think of themselves as Nigerians first, rather
than as Yoruba.

The Rise of the Muslim-Christian Conflict in Nigeria

The Spread of Christianity and Western Education in Northern Nigeria
Muslim leaders in northern Nigeria used well the initial political
advantage given them by the British, thus assuming political
domination of the country. They also used Islam as a powerful
instrument for political expansion, in accordance with the Islamic
tradition of fusing politics with religion. During the First Nigerian Republic, they pursued the policy known as "One North, One
Islam," sometimes simply called "the northernization policy,"
which aimed at unifying all northern Muslims through the agencies of the Jama'atu Nasril Islam (JNI—Society for the Victory of
Islam) and the Kaduna Council of Malams. Ahmadu Bello, the
sardauna of Sokoto and leader of the Northern Peoples Congress
(NPC), personally led a strong "islamization campaign" that
earned for Islam hundreds of thousands of new converts.[4]

But the northernization policy and the vision of "One North,
One People, and One Destiny" suffered a major setback with the
military intervention of 1966, the abolition of the regional system,
and the subsequent creation of states out of the former regions.
This process was followed by the rapid spread of Christianity and
Western education in the north, particularly in Kaduna, Plateau,
Benue, and Gongola states.

One must recognize that Islam is not just a religion; it is a way of life. The spread of a rival faith in a predominantly Muslim society is therefore perceived as a serious threat to Islamic culture, including its politics, economics, and education. For instance, Nigerian Muslims have complained endlessly about what they regard as the corrupting influence of Western education on Muslim society. Most Christians hardly realize that Islam places great emphasis on education, nor do they recognize the high level of literacy that prevails among Muslims. "Literacy," according to John Paden, "is regarded as a primary means of religious communication."[5] Yet many Nigerian Muslims have been described as backward and illiterate simply because they were not brought up in the English educational tradition—even though, as John Hunwick observes, these same people "may be able to read and write Arabic with ease and perhaps also express their mother tongue with the help of Arabic characters and may have been receiving instruction since childhood in a system which had its origins in Fez and Cairo a thousand years ago." Before the arrival of Europeans in Africa, he goes on, Muslims represented the educated elite of the society; they possessed a technological instrument—writing—that non-Muslims coveted, and they belonged to "an intellectual tradition of West Africa which studied Logic and Prosody as well as the legal and theological sciences."[6]

The sensibilities of many Nigerian Muslims are offended when they find themselves marginalized and discriminated against because they have not acquired sufficient skills in the English language, the official language of Nigeria. Their protest against this discrimination and the disruptiveness of Western education and morality on the Islamic community is illustrated by their ongoing attack on the universal primary education (UPE) scheme, which was intended to "bridge the gap between the north and the south." This scheme, they declare, is a conspiracy to destroy Islamic education and disorganize the entire Muslim community of Nigeria by producing children with little knowledge of Islamic morality, who would wear trousers, smoke, and even drink. The UPE scheme, they say, is draining Qur'anic schools of pupils, depriving Qur'anic teachers of their means of livelihood, robbing women in *kulle* (seclusion) of their errand boys and girls, and depriving blind beggars of guides. What is being imparted at the UPE schools, they have no doubt, is but a subtle form of Christian indoctrination.7

The Resurgence of Islamic Fundamentalism

Perhaps more disruptive of Christian-Muslim accord in Nigeria is the rise of Islamic fundamentalism, which in turn is related to the spread of Saudi Arabian imperialism, the recent world oil crisis, Nigeria's membership in OPEC, and, generally, the reaction of the Muslim states in the Persian Gulf and the Middle East to the spread of Western influences. An important landmark in this Islamic reaction to westernization was the removal of the pro-American shah of Iran by a Shi'ite-inspired movement and the subsequent installation of the fundamentalist Ayatollah Khomeini. The success achieved by the Ayatollah's revolution is regarded as a standard to be emulated in other parts of the Islamic world. Since the 1970s, consequently, fundamentalist Muslim sects have intensified their opposition, not only to westernization, but also to leaders they consider errant Muslims, such as Anwar el-Sadat, the president of Egypt, who was assassinated in 1981 by members of a fundamentalist group. Since then Islamic fundamentalist agitations have occurred throughout much of the Muslim world, with not even the holy places of Saudi Arabia having been spared. These groups are convinced that there is a global attack on Islam and they are determined to resist it. The ongoing Palestinian-Israeli conflict and the emergence of global terrorism and counterviolence are two current expressions of this sense of being under attack.

Although Nigerian Muslims have been performing the pilgrimage to Mecca for many centuries, the recent world oil crisis and Nigeria's membership in OPEC have brought them closer to Saudi Arabia. Following the unwelcome drop in Nigerian oil revenues in 1980–82, Saudi Arabia and some Gulf states signed a loan agreement for $1 billion for Nigeria. Although this loan was intended as assistance to a "sister Muslim country," its underlying reason was to stop Nigeria from reducing the price of its crude oil, which would have resulted in a price war among the OPEC countries. As Peter Clarke and Ian Linden have rightly pointed out, "the loan tied Nigeria more firmly to the epicentre of the Muslim universe, Saudi Arabia, and had an important symbolic dimension."[8]

Over the past few years Nigerian Muslim leaders have consciously tried to promote stronger ties between Nigeria and Saudi Arabia at a governmental level. It is believed that Saudi Arabia has responded favorably by sending large sums of money for the promotion of Islam: large amounts of Islamic literature have been circulating freely in Nigeria; mosques and Muslim schools have been built and scholarships awarded with Saudi funds; and Muslim teachers have been recruited and supported with funds from Saudi Arabia. (Most of these charges, however, have been denied.)[9]

The most active agents of Saudi imperialism in Nigeria are the various Islamic fundamentalist groups, notably the members of the Muslim Students Society (MSS) and the Yan Izala. Working largely at the institutions of higher learning, these activitists are committed to the complete islamization of Nigeria and its incorporation into the Islamic world. With talk of "dismantling the barrier created by the geographical factor between the Muslims in the South and the North," they are poised for open confrontation with Nigerian Christians in their desire to forge "a united front against Christian missionary expansion."[10]

The Muslim Students Society has an interesting history. Although it is today most active in northern Nigeria, the society was in fact born in the south. At first a predominantly Yoruba organization, it was founded in 1954 in Lagos, and two years later it became centered at the University of Ibadan, with branches later opened at Ahmadu Bello University in Zaria and Abdullahi Bayero College in Kano. In September 1969, the national convention of the society elected as president a Hausa student at Bayero College—the first non-Yoruba national president. By 1970 the society had four hundred branches throughout Nigeria, based in postprimary schools and universities, with the initiative for steering society affairs now firmly placed among northern students. Today the society is so strong that virtually all the students of Bayero University in Kano are said to be members.[11]

Some Nigerian political leaders have advised members of the MSS to be tolerant and understanding in their dealings with Christians. Aminu Kano once reminded them that much of the modernization that has taken place in the Christian world was due to education and advised them to work hand in hand with Christians to modernize Nigeria. Even the JNI has had the good sense to dissociate itself "from an emotional approach to religion and . . . stressed the importance of modern education in the northern states."[12] The MSS, however, apparently has no patience for compromises or cooperation; rather, it prefers violent confrontation in its dealings with Christians.

Perhaps no less militant than the MSS is the Yan Izala, created around 1980 by followers of Alhaji Abubakar Gummi. Like Gummi, the Izala believe in the transformation of Nigeria (or more accurately, certain parts of Nigeria) into an Islamic state. Gummi himself has called for the establishment of a ministry of religion and greater governmental interference in religion because, in his opinion, "people should not be left without spiritual guidance." The Izala oppose the use or display of certain national symbols, such as the national flag, the national anthem, and the Nigerian coat of arms, as contrary to the teachings of Islam; moreover, like many orthodox Muslims, they do not believe that one should bow down to a mortal being as is the practice at the courts of Muslim emirs. The Izala, according to Gummi, is not an Islamic sect but simply a group of people who wish to educate others, purify Islam, and fight ignorance among Muslims.[13]

If the activities of Muslim fundamentalists on the campuses were restricted to nonviolent promotion of scholarship and religion, perhaps Nigerians would have been spared a great deal of trouble. In fact, however, their religious intolerance and misplaced radicalism have earned them a bad name. Obsessed with the illusion that Nigeria is, or should be, an Islamic state, they find it difficult to see the viewpoint of non-Muslims. Their spirit of defiance, even against constituted authorities, was demonstrated in 1986 when some activists decided to seize the Ahmadu Bello University mosque in Zaria; they were subsequently removed by the Nigerian police.[14] That same year, some MSS members at the University of Ibadan insisted that the cross of a Christian church built over thirty years earlier be removed because it obstructed their view when they looked toward Mecca, though they prayed in a mosque built only in 1986. "This flagrant demand embarrassed the nation," lamented A. I. Asiwaju[15]—but no sooner had the matter been settled than some unknown persons set fire to the wooden sculpture of the risen Christ in the Protestant Christian chapel on the campus.

Christian Fundamentalism in Nigeria

The unity of Nigeria has been disturbed equally by the activities of Christian fundamentalists. There are now over one thousand independent Christian sects in Nigeria, many of them exhibiting certain fundamentalist traits.[16] The older churches, especially the Roman Catholic, Anglican, Baptist, and Methodist, are losing their flock to new fundamentalist movements. To arrest this drift, some of these older denominations have introduced elements of fundamentalism or charismatism into their mode of worship and evangelicalism. Speaking in tongues, belief in spiritual healing, insistence on baptism by immersion, and heated disputes over minutiae of Christian doctrines are but some of the traits that set the fundamentalists apart from other Christians.

Christian fundamentalism is widespread among minority ethnic groups, mainly in the Middle Belt, Cross River, and Bendel states. While there is no clear explanation for this trend, we do know that Nigerian fundamentalist groups, generally called born-again Christians, campus crusaders, and Jesus people, have their roots not in Nigeria, but in the United States and Britain; therefore, they could be regarded as belonging to the broad

Euro-American fundamentalist movement and, indeed, as the agents of Western cultural imperialism in Nigeria.

As Flo Conway and Jim Siegelman remind us, Christian fundamentalism, as "reactionary evangelicalism and as an organized movement against secularism, is a twentieth-century American invention, different from the non-conformist European sects—the old-world breakaway groups—and the Pentecostals, which were born of theological disputes over such issues as ecclesiastical rules and infant baptism."[17] Believing that Americans are God's modern-day "chosen people," militant American fundamentalists have been invading the world with their propaganda since the 1960s, with the weaker nations of Africa and Asia suffering the most from this onslaught. Captivated by the image of material plenty, of the American "good life" as portrayed in motion pictures, television, radio, books, and magazines, some Third World people easily fall prey to fundamentalist propaganda.[18] Millions of Nigerians watch the television program sponsored by Club 700 of America, for example, and large amounts of gospel tracts and pamphlets from the United States circulate freely in Nigeria.

The American brand of Christian fundamentalism has gained wide acceptance in Nigeria because of the present economic difficulties. Believing that "Jesus is the answer" to all their problems, millions of Nigerian youths become born-again Christians and surrender their lives to him. They then join the conversion "crusades," using the fundamentalists' propaganda strategy developed in the United States to win converts.

Our knowledge of the Christian fundamentalist movements in Nigeria and their political ideologies is limited. One of the best known, however, is the movement known as the Fellowship of Christian Students (FCS), which Paul Lubeck describes as a "fundamentalist Christian movement among the minority ethnic groups of Nigeria's Middle Belt."[19] Although this description suggests that the association is a Middle Belt affair, Raymond Hickey has noted that after its formation in 1957 the FCS spread quickly throughout the entire old Northern Region.[20] Just how widely spread *is* the movement? And what are its dominant political and religious ideologies?

Like the Muslim Students Society, the FCS has interesting origins. It was founded in Gindiri, near Jos—that is, not in the predominantly Christian south of Nigeria, but in the north—by the
staff of the Sudan United Mission schools, most of whom were
expatriates from Europe and America. From there the activities of
the society spread to other parts of the north, and within five years
it had fifty active branches and a full-time traveling secretary. By
1967 the society had over one hundred branches and a Nigerian
full-time general secretary. In all the areas where it was established, the society "kept pace with the rapid development of
schools and, with the cooperation of Christian staff members, it
has proved to be an effective means of protecting the faith of
Christian students in a Muslim environment. It is also an active
apostolic force among staff and students."[21]

Nurtured in a hostile environment, the FCS soon became the
vanguard of Middle Belt nationalism. As we have seen, the introduction of Christianity in northern Nigeria was opposed by Muslim rulers and colonial administrators. "That the emirs and holy
men of Islam would not welcome the establishment of a Christian
mission in their area is wholly understandable and normal,"
noted Hickey. "What is much harder to understand is the blind
opposition of many senior officers of the British colonial administration to the establishment of missions, even among the non-
Muslim communities of the region." Perhaps, Hickey suggests,
the hostility of British officials toward Christian missionaries
derived from their "almost mystical veneration . . . for both the
Sokoto caliphate and the sacrosanct system of Indirect Rule
which helped to perpetuate and fossilize a feudal society"—an
attitude that was often summed up in the expression "the Muslim
north" or, as Sir Rex Niven puts it in his recent memoirs, "the holy
and undivided North."[22]

Christian missionaries struggled against these odds and eventually became established in many parts of the north, but they
were never able to free themselves of Muslim hostility. Today, as
a consequence, the greatest areas of religious tension between
Muslims and Christians are not such predominantly Muslim
states as Sokoto, Kano, and Bornu, but the Middle Belt, which

Paul Lubeck has described as "one of the last frontiers of universalistic religious competition for converts."[23]

Besides religion, two other sources of tension mark the Middle Belt, one economic, the other political. Muslims are the dominant economic class: they are well-to-do cattle keepers and owners of the major retail outlets, road haulage companies, and contracting firms, whereas Christians are mostly peasant farmers and laborers. Politically, too, Muslims constitute the ruling class. The practice of imposing Muslim emirs on both Muslim and non-Muslim communities, which had its origins in the days of the nineteenth-century jihads and continued into the early colonial period, has remained in force despite protests by many communities and even by well-meaning Muslims. Alhaji Abubakar Gummi, for instance, has described the emirate system as a political-religious dynastic system that has no relevance for modern Nigeria: "The emirs can't continue. In fact the system has already ended."[24] Likewise, the members of the Muslim Committee for Progressive Nigeria and other socialist associations have attacked the emirate system, describing the emirs as feudal lords who "keep the majority of the poor and oppressed peasants and workers down."[25]

It is not surprising that Kaduna should be the most religiously and politically troubled state of Nigeria, for here religious, class, and political cleavages are manifested largely along ethnic lines. The Hausa-Fulani, who are mostly Muslims, constitute the dominant political and economic classes, while the Kaje and a host of other ethnic groups are mainly Christians and the subdominant classes. Note that although Kaduna State proper is not normally regarded as a part of the Middle Belt, its southern parts (known as Southern Zaria) are so considered; indeed, they share a common historical experience with the other peoples of the Middle Belt, being, for instance, the victims of Fulani military imperialism in the nineteenth century and of Hausa-Fulani political domination and economic exploitation in the twentieth.[26] Furthermore, it is in Kaduna State that the members of the fundamentalist Muslim and Christian groups, the MSS and the FCS respectively, are most active.

The bloody conflicts between these two militant societies in 1987 were not entirely unexpected. They had previously clashed and have continued to clash in almost all the institutions of higher learning in Kaduna State. At the Ahmadu Bello University their conflicts are now endemic, with the student union elections usually regarded as occasions for physical combat between these two mutually antagonistic groups. The Kaduna State religious riots of 1987 started at the College of Education in Kafanchan, when some members of the MSS argued that a Christian preacher, Rev. A. Bako, himself a recent convert from Islam, had no authority to translate verses from the Qur'an into English at a Christian religious meeting. They also accused Rev. Bako of misrepresenting the Qur'an, on account of which they tried to kill him.[27] As the preacher personally testified, "the MSS members who had already come near enough, started hitting me with clubs, sticks, and some were using stones to hit me. I just closed my eyes, since my hands were tightly held down."[28] He was, however, rescued by the timely intervention of the Christian students, who beat off the Muslim attackers.

The fight over Rev. Bako's right to quote from the Qur'an soon turned into a riot that spilled into the township and adjoining villages. A few days later, the entire Kaduna State was gripped with fear and panic as armed Muslims roamed the streets, killing, looting, and burning. About twenty-five people were reported killed, and properties totaling millions of naira were destroyed, mostly Christian churches and schools, hotels, private homes, and automobiles.[29] The Christians managed to damage only about six mosques. The greatest destruction took place in Zaria, where, according to one source, as many as 102 churches were razed to the ground.[30]

Islamic Millenarianism as a Factor in the Political Instability of Nigeria: The Case of the Maitatsine Religious Riot

Equally disruptive of the peace and stability of Nigeria are the activities of a long list of self-proclaimed Muslim prophets and reformists, the most recent being Malam Muhammadu Marwa, known as Maitatsine. In 1980 in Kano, in the very heart of the Muslim north, Nigerians of all religious affiliations were made to taste the bitter pills of religious intolerance and fanaticism when the followers of Maitatsine caused the deaths of between four thousand and six thousand people. Maitatsine was a Cameroonian who, under unknown circumstances, established himself in Kano and surrounded himself with a large number of followers—over ten thousand in Kano alone before the 1980 outbreak, reportedly. He was also believed to have followers in all the major towns of the north and, strangely, in Lagos as well. Although Maitatsine died during the Kano religious riots of 1980, his organization survived.

In 1982, his followers struck in Bulumkutu on the outskirts of Maiduguri and also in Kaduna, causing the loss of about 400 lives. Many of the fanatics were rounded up by government forces, but this did not check the sect's activities. Barely two years later they struck again in Jimeta in Gongola State; 760 were killed. Again in 1985, they attacked their real and imaginary enemies in Gombe, Bauchi State, causing the deaths of over 100 people. Later that same year the fanatics assembled in Lagos to unleash their terror on that city, but members of the armed forces arrived in time and rounded up over six thousand of them.

Muhammadu Marwa started preaching in Kano in the early 1960s. Although very little is known about the religious and political ideologies of his sect, from Marwa's own utterances it can be inferred that the organization was reformist. As Paul Lubeck explains, he "condemned the widespread corruption of existing secular and religious elites and especially the orgy of Western consumption enjoyed by Kano's privileged class during the brief but socially disruptive petroleum boom (1974–81)." Besides condemning both secular and religious authorities, Maitatsine criticized all those who enjoyed modern Western consumer goods—automobiles, radios, watches, televisions, even buttons. Yet Marwa also rejected some orthodox Muslim practices, such as facing toward Mecca when praying, and he rejected the authority of Hadith. Finally, the sect believed in "violent social protest during periods of social crisis."[31]

Regarding recruitment for his organization, the Justice Anio-golu Commission of Inquiry, set up by the federal government to look into the Kano disturbances, stated that the followers of Marwa were rural youths who remained unemployed after the harvest. Paul Lubeck, however, rejected this verdict on the grounds that it failed to account for the movement's historical origins, its changing material circumstances, and the cultural frustrations of Marwa's followers, who were essentially Qur'anic malams (teachers) who wandered through Muslim communities with their students seeking alms and sometimes performing practical and spiritual tasks for the host communities. The wealth that came with the Nigerian oil boom depressed the condition of the Qur'anic malams and their students and at the same time distanced them from their host communities. They were deprived of shelter, starved of alms and charity, and their status was redefined as "vagabonds and street urchins" rather than as respectable members of an Islamic community. It was from such a "displaced yet morally self-conscious group" that Maitatsine recruited his followers, concluded Lubeck.[32]

It is true that the oil boom created great social problems for Nigerians, but why would it provoke religious riots only in the Muslim north? To attribute the Maitatsine riots entirely to the postboom depression is to throw away a large portion of Nigerian history; as Clarke and Linden have rightly observed, the roots of the Maitatsine uprising "lie in the history of northern Nigeria itself. The sect showed many of the features of an Islamic millenarian tradition, and of the Mahdist movement, which was an important factor in the nineteenth century history of Islam in the region. Although disclaimed as an authentic expression of Muslim practice by the Muslim community, the Maitatsine phenomenon grew out of a Muslim tradition."[33]

What is the Islamic millenarian tradition? What is its relevance to the Maitatsine religious riots? Just as Christians believe in the second coming of Christ, so most Muslims believe in the coming of a Mahdi (God-guided One) who will bring about the victory of Islam for a millennium (thousand years) up to the Day of Judgment. Ibn Khaldūn, a great fourteenth-century writer, wrote:

It has been accepted by all Muslims in every epoch that at the end of time a man from the family of the Prophet will make his appearance, one who will strengthen Islam and make justice triumph; Muslims will follow him. He will gain dominance over the Muslim realm. He will be called the Mahdi. Following him the anti-Christ will appear, together with all the subsequent signs of the Day of Judgment. After the Mahdi Jesus will descend and kill the anti-Christ. Or Jesus will descend with the Mahdi and help him kill the anti-Christ.[34]

Over the last two hundred years, Mahdist thinking has caused great political turbulence throughout the grassland region of West Africa, from Senegal to the Sudan. It has resulted in wars of conversion, in large-scale migrations, in the establishment of Mahdist communities, and in the proclamation of certain individuals as the Mahdi. Ibn Khaldūn suggested that it is the poor and destitute ("the stupid masses") who are most influenced by Mahdist thinking;[35] it is they who easily believe and follow a man who proclaims himself a Mahdi, and it is they who show the greatest willingness to fight by his side, die, and so go straight to heaven. Oil boom or oil glut, such men were never lacking in an Islamic society. The Maitatsine religious disturbances are therefore best explained in terms of an Islamic millenarian tradition, not as a direct result of the Nigerian oil crisis. In southern Nigeria, in contrast, the victims of the oil crisis (mainly unemployed school leavers) took to armed robbery, urban thievery, and prostitution because of an existing imported Western culture of such criminal acts.[36]

The Sharia Debate

The first major direct confrontation between Nigerian Muslims and Christians in recent years occurred between 1976 and 1978 when the Muslims proposed the establishment of a Federal Sharia Court of Appeal. In a debate charged with emotion and threats, Christians and some Muslims expressed their opposition, whereas other Muslims argued that without Sharia "their basic way of life would not be guaranteed" and they would not feel they were practicing their religion completely.[37] Indeed, without Sharia, they warned, there would be no freedom of religion and, in the end, "no peace in Nigeria." Sharia, in their view, was necessary "for national unity."[38]

On the other hand, Christians argued that the proposal was an attempt to islamize Nigeria and perpetuate Muslim hegemony. Some disguised their opposition in nonreligious terms of political stability and national integration; some, on humanitarian grounds, objected to a legal system so oppressive of women. Others wondered why Nigerians should desire a legal system that prescribed chopping off peoples' hands for theft, public flogging for drinking as little as a glass of beer, and public stoning for adultery, when in fact theft (including the embezzlement of public funds), drinking (even among Muslims), and adultery were regarded as national pastimes. Some Nigerian radicals, too, denounced the Sharia proposal on nonreligious grounds. For example, the Muslim Committee for Progressive Nigeria and other socialist associations described Sharia law as "the most backward Muslim religious, legal and customary instrument in the hands of the minority of feudal emirs for keeping the majority of the poor and oppressed peasants and workers down."[39]

On the whole, the rejection of Sharia was based on four major contentions: Sharia was but part of a great design to islamize Nigeria and entrench northern (Muslim) domination; because section 17 of the draft constitution stated that Nigeria shall not adopt any religion as the state religion, it was ridiculous for the government to single out Islam for special treatment; because only part of the Nigerian population was Muslim, it would be unfair for the federal government to spend the taxpayers' money and time for the benefit of only that part; and if a special legal system was established for the Muslims, it might become necessary to establish another for Christians and a third for the followers of the traditional religions. Some critics drew attention to the dangers of creating dual loyalties based on religion, citing the tragic experiences of the Sudan, Lebanon, and Ireland.

The Sharia debate provoked so much controversy that many people feared it would lead to the destruction of the country. Even foreign observers predicted a bloody conflict. Some Nigerian patriots called on the military government to continue in office. "I certainly wonder if, after all, the Army should not just continue," cried Alhaji Umaru Muhammad Baba from Gongola State.[40] Yet after all the hue and cry, the proposal was dropped and the country spared a bloody conflict. It should be noted that the Sharia proposal was put aside not only because of Christian opposition but also because the Supreme Military Council, whose members were anxious to retire to the barracks or to their recently accumulated petro-naira, was determined not to allow religion to break up the country. The moderate stand of Yoruba Muslims toward the whole Sharia demand, too, may have helped to diffuse tension.[41] Nevertheless, the demand by Nigerian Muslims for a Federal Sharia Court of Appeals was never killed; it was simply swept under the carpet and has surfaced from time to time over the last ten years.

The Organization of Islamic Conference

The historical importance of the Sharia debate lies in the fact that thenceforth Nigerian Christians were suspicious of almost any moves, no matter how well intentioned, the Muslims might be contemplating. No wonder, then, that in 1986, when the federal government announced that Nigeria had been admitted into the Organization of Islamic Conference (OIC), many Christians raised their voices in opposition, calling the move a renewed attempt to islamize the country. Even some Muslims opposed Nigeria's admission; for example, Chief Sule Oyesola Gbadamosi of Ikorodu, a man described as a strong Muslim and a successful industrialist, is said to have called the move an exhibition of "downright dishonesty which is contrary to the teaching of the Holy Prophet."[42] So much unnecessary ill will was caused that the then military governor of Kaduna State, Lt. Col. Abubakar Umar, branded the OIC issue as responsible for a new religious mistrust in the country: "The Christians think that by joining the OIC they would lose out," he said, "and the Muslims believe that by not belonging . . . they would lose out."[43]

Indeed, the Christians had reason to fear that they would "lose out." The United Christian Association of Oyo State, an affiliate

of the Christian Association of Nigeria, charged that article 8 of
the OIC charter, dealing with membership, presumed that all
member states were Islamic; that article 2, section A(i), declared
that the major aspiration of the OIC was "to promote Islamic solidarity among member States"; and that since the OIC was an
association based on religion, its interests were at variance with
the aspirations of Nigeria, a secular state. The association also
noted that article 4 of the OIC charter implied that all future
Nigerian heads of state and ministers of external affairs had to be
Muslims, and that article 7(i), in stating that "all expenses of the
administration and activities of the secretariat shall be borne by
member-states according to their national incomes," implied that
Nigeria's resources would be used to propagate the course of
Islam.[44]

In addition, Nigeria's admission into the OIC raised such
thorny questions as Nigeria's future relationship with Israel; what
role Nigerians would play in the event of a war between the Arabs
and, say, the United States, the Soviet Union, or Western Europe;
and whether Nigeria's status as a nonaligned nation would be
affected.

Observers regarded the settlement of the OIC controversy as
one of President Ibrahim Babangida's tests of statesmanship. Sens-
ing that the dispute might divide the nation, he decided to kill it
by adopting a strategy that has been described as "keeping people
guessing, and staying one jump ahead." Thus, just as the president temporarily got Nigerians out of the IMF trap, so he led
them out of the OIC controversy simply by announcing that
Nigeria's membership had been suspended.[45] In the final analysis,
though, the OIC issue, like the Sharia debate before it, has yet to
be permanently resolved.

Conclusion

This paper has identified three broad causes of Muslim-Christian
conflict in Nigeria: the resurgence of rival fundamentalist and
reformist ideologies; the spread of Saudi Arabian and Western
cultural imperialism; and the politicization and manipulation of
religion by some Nigerian political entrepreneurs. The disputes

over Sharia and the OIC are mere manifestations and not the cause of the conflict. Perhaps, rather than ethnicity, regionalism, and official corruption, it is religion that poses the greatest threat to Nigeria's political survival and stability in the 1990s. The Babangida administration has proposed a two-party system when Nigeria returns to civilian rule in 1992, but it is difficult to see how the new parties will not be influenced by the two major religions or how the conflict between Muslims and Christians will not escalate as each group tries to gain control of the government and resources.

Between eight thousand and ten thousand people were killed in the first seven years of this decade as a result of religious disturbances in Nigeria. To avert further bloodshed and the possible breakup of the country, the people and government of Nigeria must make urgent and conscious efforts to diffuse the current religious tension. Nigerians need to realize that any society that draws its entire inspiration from religion, whether traditional or universalistic, lives in the past. Such a society progresses in a cyclical fashion, living under the same old economic, legal, and political systems, and, in concrete terms, achieves nothing. Whereas modern societies excel in the fields of art, science, and technology, religious societies strive endlessly to live according to divine and unchanging laws (as revealed by the *juju* priests or God's prophets). Likewise, Nigerians need to realize that the country is a multireligious nation. Anyone who still dreams of imposing either an Islamic or a Christian code on Nigeria is living in the distant past. The age of forced conversions, of jihads and crusades, is over.

Fortunately, hard-line Muslim and Christian fanatics, fundamentalists, and political opportunists constitute but a small percentage of the Nigerian population. The minority view must not be allowed to prevail over the majority wisdom; Nigerians must not succumb to fundamentalists' blackmail, be it Islamic or Christian. There are large groups of Muslims and Christians ready to work together to build a progressive Nigeria. While the federal government should encourage them, at the same time it should refrain from financing religious projects and activities; by the same token, state and federal governments should cease maintaining religious traditional rulers with public funds.

The public must be educated to the fact that religion is a private matter and that in a multireligious society government cannot afford to identify with a particular faith or sect. All political parties should be founded on political and economic ideologies, not on religious ideologies. The political catastrophe that looms so menacingly over Nigeria can be averted only by curtailing the involvement of religious entrepreneurs in national politics and by arresting the current spread of communal violence inspired by religion. Similarly, under no circumstances should politicians be allowed to mobilize or manipulate religion for own their private ends.

Notes

1 On the last point, see Yusuf Bala Usman, *The Manipulation of Religion in Nigeria, 1977–1987* (Kaduna: Vanguard, 1987).

2 John N. Paden, *Religion and Political Culture in Kano* (Berkeley and Los Angeles: University of California Press, 1973), 49; Peter B. Clarke and Ian Linden, *Islam in Modern Nigeria: A Study of a Muslim Community in a Post-Independence State, 1960–1983* (Mainz: Grünewald, 1983), 49–50.

3 See, generally, David Laitin, *Hegemony and Culture: Politics and Religious Change Among the Yoruba* (Chicago: University of Chicago Press, 1986).

4 Paden, *Religion and Political Culture*, 47–48.

5 Ibid., p. 139.

6 John Hunwick, *Literacy and Scholarship in Muslim West Africa in the Precolonial Period* (Nsukka: Institute of African Studies, University of Nigeria, 1974), 9.

7 Clark and Linden, *Islam in Modern Nigeria*, 151–54.

8 Ibid., 62.

9 Ibid., 65–66.

10 Ibid., 50.

11 Paden, *Religion and Culture*, 206.

12 Ibid., 207.

13 On Yan Izala generally, see *Newswatch*, 30 March 1987, 17, box "Sheikh Abubakar Gummi."

14 Ibid., 13.

15 A. I. Asiwaju, Review of Laitin's *Hegemony and Culture*, *West Africa*, 3 August 1987, 1489.

16 See Rosalind I. J. Hackett, *New Religious Movements in Nigeria* (Lewiston, [N.Y.]: E. Mellen Press, [1987]).

17 Flo Conway and Jim Siegelman, *Holy Terror: The Fundamentalist War on American Freedoms in Religion, Politics, and Private Lives* (New York: Doubleday, 1982), 199. See also Jerry Falwell with Ed Dobson and Ed Hinson, *The Fundamentalist Phenomenon: The Resurgence of Conservative Christianity* (New York: Doubleday, 1981).

18 Conway and Siegelman, *Holy Terror*, 202.

19 Paul Lubeck, "Populism, Islamization, and Political Realignment in Nigeria," Paper presented at a seminar organized by the Humanities Center, Stanford University, Stanford, 18 May 1988, 15.

20 Raymond Hickey, *Christianity in Borno State and Northern Gongola* (Aachen, Ger., 1984), 45.

21 Ibid.

22 Quoted in ibid., v.

23 Lubeck, "Populism, Islamization, and Political Realignment," 15.

24 Lee Lescaze, "Nigerian Stability Threatened by Schism Among Moslems," *Wall Street Journal,* 13 March 1987, 16.

25 As quoted in Clarke and Linden, *Islam in Modern Nigeria,* 88–89.

26 For an account of how the labor force of the Middle Belt communities was plundered by northern emirs acting as agents of European colonial officials and investors, see, for instance, Bill Freund, *Capital and Labour in the Nigerian Tin Mines* (London: Longman, 1981); and Michael Mason, "Working on the Railway: Forced Labour in Northern Nigeria, 1907–1911," in Peter C. W. Gutkind, Robin Cohen, and Jean Copans (eds.), *African Labor History* (Beverly Hills, Calif.: Sage, 1978), 56–79.

27 Christian Association of Nigeria, *Kaduna Religious Riot, 1987: A Catalogue of Events* (Kaduna, n.d.), 21, 18.

28 Ibid., 11.

29 *Newswatch,* 30 March 1987, 20.

30 Christian Association of Nigeria, *Kaduna Religious Riot,* 67.

31 Paul Lubeck, "Islamic Protest Under Semi-industrial Capitalism: Yan Tatsine Explained," *Africa* 55 (1985): 370.

32 Ibid., 371, 377–85.

33 Clarke and Linden, *Islam in Modern Nigeria,* 109.

34 Quoted in ibid., 109.

35 Ibid., 109.

36 For an interesting account and dramatization of the relationships between the Nigerian oil boom and armed robbery, see Karin Barber, "Popular Reaction to the Petro-Naira," *Journal of Modern African Studies* 20 (1982): 431–50.

37 David Laitin, "The Sharia Debate and the Origins of Nigeria's Second Republic," *Journal of Modern African Studies* 20 (1982): 418. See also W. I. Ofonagoro et al. (eds.), *The Great Debate: Nigerian Viewpoints on the Draft Constitution, 1976–1977* (Lagos: Daily Times of Nigeria, n.d.).

38 Laitin, "Sharia Debate," 418.

39 Clarke and Linden, *Islam in Modern Nigeria,* 57.

40 Laitin, "Sharia Debate," 417.

41 Ibid., 429–30.

42 *West Africa,* 3 August 1987, 1489–90.

43 *West Africa,* 16 November 1987, 2245.

44 United Christian Association of Oyo State, *The Christian and the OIC* (n.p., n.d.), 1.

45 *West Africa,* 30 March 1987, 599.

Commentary on the Papers of Ibrahim Gambari and Don Ohadike, Followed by General Discussion

Commentary by David Laitin

In terms of the title of this conference, I am not comfortable with the concept of "national integration." Nor do I know if it is a good thing. Mr. Gambari in his final comments suggested that national integration seems to mean that we all become something like each other. That may not be a good thing.

The question that interests me is the symbolic basis of political conflict: On what cultural dimensions will people divide, and what are the consequences for those types of divisions? (That is, assuming people will divide on the basis of their differences for purposes of political action and that that is a normal part of political life.) In regard to this theme, my first point is that complexity is not something that is unique to the Sudan or Nigeria, but complexity is a universal characteristic of societies and states. To point out that one's own country is complex is merely to say that one knows it better than others and one sees the divisions within it more clearly. Not only is complexity universal, but so are tolerance and intolerance. I do not believe that there are societies that are more tolerant and societies that are less tolerant than others. In fact, I believe, people are tolerant about some sorts of things and intolerant about others. In my own research in Nigeria I remember interviewing the chief imam of a Friday mosque and telling him about my views on religious conflict. He said, "Well, those people who engage in religious conflict are morally intolerant people. Islam teaches us to be tolerant." I then asked him about what was going on at another Friday mosque that was patronized by Muslims who came from a different, you might say, ancestral city from the ancestral city of the chief imam with whom I was speaking. Suddenly his blood began to boil telling me that those people at the other mosque had no sense of honor and that they were thoroughly reprehensible people. It is not that he was more tolerant than people in the Middle East in seeing a role for Christianity in Nigeria. Rather, he was tolerant about a religious division, but intolerant about an ancestral city division. So the point I want to make is that all societies have complex cultural tapestries and that in all societies people are tolerant about some sorts of divisions and intolerant about others, and that the consequences of those choices between what you are tolerant and intolerant about and how the complex society divides itself politically is what political scientists and sociologists study. As I am one of them, I have some thoughts on this.

As political leaders or putative political leaders seek to gain political power, they need to in some way connect with their own mass base. We know from our studies of leadership and their followership and how this dynamic interaction works that it is very easy to appeal to a common identity between leader and follower, and you emphasize those aspects in which you have some common feeling whether it be religion, region, language, tribe, history, or skin color. You try to connect in some way with the constituency that you want to build. That is in a sense an instrument for mobilization by leaders, but leaders are not completely free to use it; as we say in America, it has to play in Peoria.

Once a leader develops some kind of followership based on this common sense of identity, there is a problem because, as I said, societies are complex and, as Mr. Abu-Lughod was saying earlier, no one sees himself so clearly. Everyone sees himself as a layered person with all sorts of connections, going back to your grandfather, great-grandfather, or your mother's family, or something like that. Virtually anyone can think of a number of identities one has and why one is connected to the group that one is supposed to oppose in some way. What leaders try to do, in the words of a political scientist at the University of Washington, Paul Brass, in his magnificent study of language and religion in north India, is to create some degree of "symbolic congruence." Once you have your following, you try to make it seem that the boundaries between you and your opposition are far more solid than they really are sociologically. So when it was said earlier, especially in the Sudan lectures, that the leadership emphasizes the clarity of the boundaries between groups when in fact the world is more complex, this is rather a common political phenomenon and an incentive for leadership to engage in creating some congruence to show that the group has coherence—trying to develop a coherent notion of what you are. So if your dominant symbolic message is based on language you try to make the religious differences among your language group appear irrelevant. "We are very tolerant about religion, but it is our language group which is central to our political claims."

If there is success by leadership (not all leaders succeed in creating a followership with clear boundaries and devotion to that scheme of things from the cultural point of view that the leader has developed), if there is success in this project of leaders and followers to create a political group, in some sense we can say there has been established in the society, using Marshall Sahlins's phrase, a "dominant cultural framework." That dominant cultural framework we will call hegemonic if behind it is political and economic power in the process of state formation.

In Nigeria, Lord Lugard was instrumental in bringing about this kind of symbolic congruence, this kind of dominant cultural framework. It looked something like this: the north was basically Muslim, that was what their real identity was. All those other differences up there were differences to be sure—economic and language, historical differences. Middle Belt people did not fit into that at all, but we will just sort of forget about that. The dominant identification in the north was that they are all Muslims, which differentiated them from the south. Lord Lugard also wrote, and acted on these writings, that the south was not advanced enough to make religion its dominant symbolic framework. They were still at the historical evolutionary stage of being based on the tribe. Therefore, people making claims based on religion in the south were in some way socially jumping and those kinds of claims were not to be heard or officially recognized. That is overstating it some, but the image of the Muslim north and the tribal south was one that Lugard tried to promote not because it was real, but because it was plausible enough for people to act strategically and think and organize according to the dimensions set up by the British imperial state.

As Mr. Gambari pointed out, there was a set of historical compromises in the postindependence Nigerian state that in a sense challenged the colonial hegemony. The twelve-state system of the Gowan period broke up the north. Once the north was broken up into more than one state, the fissures between northerners especially, and also between the northerners and the people of the Middle Belt, broke the ideology of the sardauna of a united Muslim north. Second, the civil war ended the view that there was a three-tribe Nigeria and the notion that the Yoruba were the central tribe of the west, the Ibo the central tribe in the east, and something called Hausa-Fulani—whatever that means—the central tribe in the north.

We can say that in the post–civil war period there has been a punctured hegemony in Nigeria. By that I mean to say that there is no form of cultural identification which is the obvious form for purposes of political action. In a sense, this punctured hegemony works to the interest of the regime in Nigeria because the available frameworks may prove insufficient for leadership to develop an effective followership. Developing a dominant cultural framework on which to base political action in contemporary Nigeria will be difficult because organizing on the basis of tribe is very difficult. Why? Because the number of people who recognize themselves as different tribes is so high you have to build an enormous coalition of tribes. Once you build an enormous coalition of tribes, the notion of what they share is so loose that it is hard to get that kind of symbolic attachment with the people. So tribe becomes a very weak form of countering the dominance of the ruling group. How about class? Class is also a tremendous problem, in large part because of the, you might say, petty bourgeois aspiration of virtually every social group in Nigeria or every region in Nigeria. If people saw themselves as permanent workers, as Europeans did in the nineteenth century—the children of the working class likely to be working class in turn—then the idea that you have working-class interests for purposes of political identification seems plausible. In Nigeria, after one or two generations of working class everyone sees himself breaking out of that and owning something, getting the Mercedes Benz distributorship. Then the effort to bring about some form of working-class consciousness will have all gone in vain.

Religion has become a new, you might say, ploy or a new attempt because, as has been recognized by Mr. Gambari, the tremendous social inequalities, especially in urban areas, are so great and so egregious that there has to be some mechanism to mobilize discontent. Religious leaders come along and have been so far, in the last few years, much more successful, especially Mai Tatsine in the north, much more successful than tribal leaders in mobilizing this urban discontent. However, here is where I disagree with the earlier speakers just a bit. This is not so ominous. If you think about it, religious differences so cross-cut the discontent that it would be very difficult to build up a massive organization of the discontent based on some religious symbols. In the north, the discontent are basically Muslim; in the south, they are both Muslim and Christian. The question of the Aladura groups in the south coalescing with the discontent among the Anglicans is very low probability. So the chance of building a religious-based movement that transcends one locality in Nigeria seems to me very low and seems to me to explain why these last riots were contained within Kaduna State—because of the fact of discontent cross-cutting religion. The one piece of evidence that I have to support my view here, that even though religion has been used—and more successfully than tribe, I do admit—for purposes of mobilizing discontent, it is not likely to become the dominant symbolic framework, is that if you looked at Yoruba Friday mosques during the Mai Tatsine movement, you would find that there was no talk there along the lines of "Look what they are doing up north and look what they are getting away with! How come we are not doing it when we are suffering as much as our brethren in the north, we Muslims in the south." So that even though religion has had some local successes in terms of mobilizing discontent, I tend to think that in Nigeria as a whole, religion as a basis for a dominant symbolic framework will not sell.

Our second speaker's idea of a Christian democratic and some kind of a Muslim party as a bipolar outcome in Nigeria I hold as highly unlikely, given the nature of social cleavages in Nigeria. So in conclusion, I think Mr. Gambari is correct in fearing the violent mobilization of discontent in Nigeria. I think that anyone who has been in Nigeria for a while, seeing the seething anger and the tremendous change in the urban areas, has to be worried about that, especially as the ruling classes seem to be so inured to the difficulties that these poor are suffering. But what its symbolic basis will be and the consequence of that choice, I contend, remains unknown.

Commentary by John O. Hunwick

It now falls to my lot to make some remarks about the situation in Nigeria and particularly about the two papers we have heard. It is very difficult to know quite where to start—there are so many complex and cross-cutting factors. But I want to start with a saying attributed to the Prophet Muhammad: *Ikhtilāf ummatī raḥma*, "Difference of opinion within my community is [a sign of] divine mercy." Perhaps we should take this as a kind of motto for both of the pluriconfessional states we are discussing today, the Sudan and Nigeria. Differences of opinion and cultural, religious, ethnic, and linguistic diversity—these kinds of things are in fact a source of blessing. They can be used as positive elements in building a modern state, and indeed, although they do not appear on the surface to be forces of integration, I believe that ultimately an honest recognition of those differences can assist in national integration.

I want to start by saying a word about that term that has been bandied about so much today—Sharia. What do we mean by Sharia? Whatever I say about it, somebody else will disagree with me, I can be pretty sure of that. There are many different possible interpretations of that term. Sharia, as far as I know, means essentially a way of life, a path, a way of Muslim life, a way of Muslims being and expressing themselves. One of the particular expressions of Sharia has been through what we call in Arabic *fiqh*, or jurisprudence—law, in a word. But there again, the situation is enormously complicated. First of all, there is the fact that law grew up and established itself over many centuries in Islam with many different interpretations, with many differing views, coalescing eventually among the Sunni majority into the four so-called legal schools, the *madhhab*s, which all have their differences one from another. Beyond this, of course, there has been continuing growth of Islamic law through the *fatwā*, the legal opinion, through the commentaries that have been made on the earlier works of jurisprudence and so on. There is an immense sort of tangled field that by itself we call Islamic law, not to speak of Sharia.

When we refer to Sharia in, say, Nigeria, again we are dealing with something different from "Sharia" as was proclaimed by Nimeiri in the Sudan. There has always been Sharia in Nigeria of a certain kind. The Muslims have been always able to follow Islamic law of the Maliki school in their personal affairs, in matters of marriage, divorce, inheritance, and so on. Prior to the colonial period, of course, Maliki law was applied more universally, though I think probably far less universally than most people suppose; in other words, I think local custom played a great role in many areas. But prior to the colonial period Sharia was dominant in many areas in the fields of criminal and commercial law as well as personal status. However, in the colonial period its jurisdiction in commercial and criminal matters was declared "null and void," and a form of law based ultimately on British law was introduced in these fields, while the Islamic personal-status law continued. So when people in Nigeria talk about Sharia law, and when they talked about it during the discussions for the constitution of the Second Republic, basically what they were talking about was not the kind of Sharia that was introduced into the Sudan, which is across the board including criminal law, including the *ḥudūd* that Mr. An-Na'im referred to—the specified punishments. They are really talking only about Muslims having the right to have their personal affairs directed by Islamic law and there being an appeals system over and above that.

Beyond this there is another kind of problem. Islamic law in some senses has never been modernized or updated. If you go to northern Nigeria, the law books, the manuals of Maliki law that are studied there in traditional circles and that are studied in places like the former School of Arabic Studies in Kano and so on, are the law books that were written in the tenth century perhaps—the *Risāla* of Ibn Abi Zayd al-Qayrawani—or the fourteenth century—the *Mukhtaṣar* of Khalil—and so on, which contain everything of legal import, including what Mr. An-Na'im was referring to about the status of non-Muslims, including all the legislation concerning slavery, et cetera. It is all there.

Now, some of these books have recently been translated into English as if this is the form of Islamic law one might want to apply in Nigeria. So you have that kind of medieval legacy of Islamic law. Nobody has yet really come up in modern times with a new interpretation of Islamic law, going back to the original sources of Islamic law and saying, "We want Islamic law, but we want an Islamic law that suits the conditions of the twentieth century. We want a new interpretation of it. We do not necessarily want an Islamic law that really reflects the economic and social conditions of the tenth century or the twelfth century." I suspect that the kind of interpretation that the late Ustadh Mahmoud Muhammad Taha in *The Second Message of Islam*, which Mr. An-Na'im has translated, attempts to solve that problem by saying essentially that much of the social legislation of the Qur'an was specific only to the time of the Prophet and is not part of the eternal message that all Muslims must follow. That was a very bold kind of statement, which was declared a "heresy" and for which of course the late ustadh paid with his life. Those kinds of bold attempt are not very common now. So the question is: When we talk about Sharia, what kind of Sharia are we talking about and how would that be interpreted? Are we going back to a medieval legacy? Are we trying to reinterpret? What are we trying to do? Nobody can really make up their minds, so people use this term across the board and it becomes a kind of bogey word—this awful thing called Sharia which nobody really ever very clearly defines. It certainly became a sort of bogey word in Nigeria: every time people heard the word *Sharia* they had visions of people being stoned to death or having their hands cut off, and so on.

One question, and I think this has already been raised, is whether interreligious rivalry or tension *is* a real and major problem in Nigeria. There are all kinds of tensions, it seems to me, going on in Nigeria, and religion sometimes merely serves as a reflection of these. For example, if you take the Yoruba people, the divisions there are not between Muslim Yoruba and Christian Yoruba, as far as I can see—and I stand to be corrected on this. There are other kinds of political division among the Yoruba, other kinds of divisions other than Muslim Yoruba versus Christian Yoruba. If we look at the kinds of tension that exist between some Muslim communities in Nigeria, again it is not as if we are dealing with a sort of monolithic block of people who are called "The Muslims of Nigeria." There is plenty of tension and unease very often between Yoruba Muslims and Hausa Muslims. This has been written about by one of the Yoruba scholars extensively, a man called Adam Abdullahi al-Iluri, who has complained bitterly that the Hausa Muslims do not treat the Yoruba Muslims as serious or genuine Muslims. So there are these kinds of tension there too. There are plenty of other kinds of tension between Muslim groups in Nigeria. For example, the sorts of tension that exist between those who are adherents of the various Sufi orders, notably the Qadiriyya and the Tijaniyya, who have their own inter-Sufi rivalries and then, as it were, jointly against those who follow what has been loosely called the "Izāla line." This is shorthand for a movement called Izālat al-bidaʿ wa-iqāmat al-sunna—"Removing of Innovation and the Establishment of the Sunna"—which in a broad sense reflects a kind of Saudi Arabian "Wahhabi" point of view that places a great deal of emphasis on the law, on Sharia—however that is to be interpreted—and tends to deny the claims of the Sufis, the mystics.

There are tensions again between most Muslims in Nigeria and the minority group called the Ahmadiyya, a sect introduced from India/Pakistan earlier in the century that caught on to a considerable extent particularly in western Nigeria. There are tensions between those who would call themselves progressive Muslims or socialist-oriented Muslims and the more traditional Muslims. These, of course, have been reflected in various kinds of political parties and political debates—the Muslim Students Association, for example, which has become a very militant sort of organization where there are pro-Iranian factions and pro-Libyan factions and so on. There again there are what we might call the middle-of-the-road Muslims in political terms, those who represent the rump of the old NPC [Northern Peoples Congress], the sardauna's party, and those who are more radicalized but still not as radicalized as the Muslim Students Association, the ex–Aminu Kano NEPU [Northern Elements Progressive Union] group. So again, there are various levels of difference of opinion and various levels of tension among the Muslims themselves.

There are also tensions, as has been mentioned in several cases, throughout Nigeria that cut across religion, region, or ethnic group, between the rural and the increasingly urban population and between the underprivileged and the elite. We have had several references to the Mai Tatsine movement as a revolt of the underprivileged against the overprivileged. There are, of course, plenty of economic grievances, particularly in the post–oil boom period. I have heard it said that the oil boom was probably the worst thing that ever happened to Nigeria. It created far more problems than it solved. One of the things I think it did was to bring Nigeria, at a certain level, much closer to the great oil powers of the Middle East, particularly to Saudi Arabia, Iran, and the Gulf states. Perhaps some of the religious tensions in Nigeria are not unconnected with this kind of closeness that Nigeria achieved at a certain level with these countries.

One could go on to the many other forms of tension that exist—the political and constitutional tension. Should Nigeria be secular or Islamic? What do we mean by secular? Many Nigerians objected during the constitutional debate when people started talking about a secular state. Muslims and Christians alike said, "We are all religious people! How can you tell us we are secular?" As if a secular state were the equivalent of an atheistic state, which of course it is not. But there was a sensitivity toward the use of the term *secularist*.

There are other kinds of tension, such as civilian/military tension, states/federal government tension. One of the continuing problems in Nigeria is determining how much power the states are to have, and how much power the federal government is to have. Or how many states should there be? Twelve, nineteen, twenty-one, or twenty-seven? How far do you go on breaking it up? Then you get back to party politics. One party? Two parties? Multiparties? Of course, Nigeria has always been a multiparty democracy when it has been a democracy, reflecting the many different points of view, the many different kinds of coalition, the careful balancing of power that goes on. One of the things one notes, however, is that none of these parties has ever been what I would call an ideological party. There has never been a Nigerian Communist party. There has never been really even a Socialist party. These kind of broader political ideologies have never taken firm root in Nigeria. Perhaps it is that people are using religion in the absence of any obvious political ideology.

In my view, and, I think, in the view of a number of the other speakers, the differences which exist between these people are not going to be resolved on a religious basis. There are just too many differences not only among the Muslims, which are the differences I have highlighted, but also equally among the Christians.

There are too many other cross-cutting factors to get any kind of monolithic Christian-versus-Muslim factionalism as a means of political expression.

Clearly, the problems that Nigeria has are no less acute than those of the Sudan. They are, I think, perhaps more easily capable of solution than some of those that exist in the Sudan in the sense that Nigeria is not currently locked into a civil war. That does make a great difference. Nigeria has been through a civil war, one that some interpreted as having some kind of religious overtones. I think that interpretation was often overblown.

Abubakar Gummi's name has been mentioned. Certainly some of the statements he has made recently have sounded somewhat alarming, indicating that if there were to be a non-Muslim head of state then Muslims would never agree to that or they would separate off. But as others have pointed out, Nigerians are often long on rhetoric and short on actual follow-through. We have all heard this kind of saber-rattling before. There is no way one can imagine the Muslims of Nigeria withdrawing from anything—or even just the north. In July 1966 there was some suggestion that the [then] Northern Region should secede, but that talk did not last very long. The sheer logistics of it, the sheer economic implications of it, militated against that. I think that Nigerians have learned that despite all their differences, their better long-term future lies in staying together and working out some kind of compromise.

Before closing I will mention briefly what I call the educational tensions in Nigeria. The love of Nigerians for education is well known, but there is of course in Nigeria, as there is in many African countries, an educational crisis. This is most clearly evident in the present state of universities in Nigeria. Many people are being half educated. People are graduating and not finding jobs. People are going anywhere to get qualifications whether relevant or irrelevant to the real needs of Nigeria. A spinoff of this is that many students have gone to the Arab countries, particularly to Saudi Arabia, which has been very generous in granting scholarships to many West Africans. So one is getting a generation of

Muslims in Nigeria and other West African countries who have received their higher education in Saudi Arabia. Of course, in any country you go to for higher education you are bound to imbibe some of the ideology and culture of that country. I think that in the case of Saudi Arabia's tremendous emphasis on the "legal way," the Sharia way, some of this has obviously worn off. People come back and they become secondary dispersion centers for ideas picked up in Saudi Arabia. Perhaps one should say thankfully that not too many went to Iran, otherwise the ideas of the Ayatollah Khomeini, which are still popular among some of the radical Muslim students, might be still more widespread.

Having mentioned the Ayatollah Khomeini, I should note that he is one of the rare examples one can find in Islamic history of a religious leader actually becoming a head of state. This is extremely uncommon in Islamic history. One can hardly find examples of men of religion becoming heads of state. They may guide the ruler, may provide an ideology, as Muhammad ibn Abd al-Wahhab did for the Saud family, or as in [eleventh-century] North Africa Abdullah ibn Yasin provided the ideology for the Almoravids while political power remained in the hands of men of politics. One of the few examples one *can* name comes from Nigeria. The movement led by Usman dan Fodio at the beginning of the nineteenth century was one of those rare movements in which the ideologue behind the revolution and behind the government became the head of state. I suspect, however, that is a direction relatively few Nigerians would see as worthwhile to go in in the twentieth century.

DISCUSSION

MR. GAMBARI: I want to respond to some of the points made by Mr. Hunwick and Mr. Laitin. Concerning Gummi and his statement that Muslims would not accept a Christian leader of Nigeria: this should be taken with a pinch of salt. Number one, we have had three Christian rulers in Nigeria, and Gummi and others did not disappear. So Gummi should be seen as an establishment malam. He has been with every conceivable government in Nigeria. He has no interest really in a situation where there would be chaos and no government. As a matter of fact, he has joined the Religious Affairs Council and has become a moderating influence there. He is quoted as having said that Christian organizations should join the Religious Affairs Council and [that] the Muslims would not mind if a Christian became the chairman.

Finally, Mr. Laitin suggested that I said that I was in favor of integration because we in Nigeria should become something like each other. I want it to be recognized that I respect differences and can take conflict so that we establish a regime of unity *and* diversity. I do believe that national integration is a good thing—at least if we look at it negatively, that national *dis*integration is not a good thing . . . [Laughter] I mean, civil wars, civil strife, boundary conflicts within states, obviously retard development and I would certainly be in favor of national integration that implies national unity even beyond the pan-African level.

Mr. Laitin also suggests that religious discontent in Nigeria is not so ominous. I think this can be underplayed—the role of religious discontent—because right there what you have is behind-the-scenes efforts, the bureaucrats, the intellectuals, the trade unions, the military itself, trying to see that religious discontent does not get out of hand. If they do not continue in such a role and they abandon the role of moderation, then you may not be able to contain religious riots territorially. Mr. Ohadike said it was a lucky thing that the religious riots were contained within Kaduna State. Suppose they could not have been contained; suppose Christians began to attack Muslims in other parts of Nigeria. This might then polarize Nigeria in a north-south divide, which I think would be very dangerous for the continued existence of Nigeria. So you are right that religious discontent is not enough to destroy Nigeria, but when it is mixed with other factors and is not contained and those who play moderating roles do not continue to do so, then we will have very serious problems.

Regarding Mr. Hunwick's points: I agree with you that the Sharia issue is not as ominous in Nigeria as is often portrayed, particularly by Christians. Sharia has been present in northern Nigeria for a long time, and it is limited to private law. Muslims were discontent when this issue of Sharia was overblown. I said, "Why cannot Muslims in the southern part of Nigeria be allowed to settle legal problems of personal status in Sharia courts in the south?" But this is strongly opposed, and the issue has not been resolved.

Further, yes, there has not been an ideological party in Nigeria, but there have been some that have come close. And I think that the more difficult the economic situation becomes in Nigeria, the more you might have more ideological parties in Nigeria in the future.

Finally, in terms of training in Iran, Mr. Hunwick said that it was a good thing that many Nigerian students have not gone to Iran and thereby taken up the Ayatollah Khomeini's religious fundamentalism. It is quite right that Nigerians will go anywhere to get an education, and an increasing number are going there . . . going to Iran, and they are returning.

MR. BESHIR: I would like to make two major comments. Regarding religion, whether it is in Nigeria or the Sudan, we seem not to have discussed this aspect very clearly. In religions, Islam and Christianity, both have extraterritorial dimensions. The question is, what has been the role and influence of outside factors in the rise of this religious movement of fundamentalism, whether in Nigeria or in the Sudan? In the Sudan we know that the international Christian organizations have played a role both in promoting conflict and in containing conflict. I must say this, they had a very positive role. They have helped in managing the conflict. The World Council of Churches, the Vatican in 1972, played a positive constructive role for the Addis Ababa agreement, and even the Emperor Haile Selassie, a Christian, played a positive role in bringing peace to the Sudan. I am saying this because the outside factor is a reality in the promotion of peace. In the present situation in the Sudan, who is doing what? Egypt has a role in the Nile Valley, so it is playing a role. Libya has a role in Chad, so it is playing a role. Ethiopia has got problems, so it is playing a role. Iran is playing a role, definitely—there is no doubt about it. Iraq is playing a role. Out-side conflicts are fanning the religious or ethnic conflicts inside the country. Whatever we are talking about, then, we have to remember these things. Also, religious organizations and fanaticism have created Islamic and Christian organizations. Ten years ago we did not have groups—associations—among University of Khartoum students; now we have them. Of course, there are outside inputs and injections promoting them, not for Sudanese interests, but for other interests.

My other comment is on the question, In the case of the Sudan or Nigeria, can religion play a role in conflict solving? We have been talking about conflict promoting. Let us ask one question: As it is presented today, can religion play a role in solving the problems? Of course, Mr. An-Na'im said this morning that it can, providing it is rightly interpreted, provided fanaticism is excluded. I agree, but others in other cases have answered the question negatively, saying that no conflict with extremist dimensions, whether religious or nationalistic, can be solved. People have answered: "Let conflicts burn themselves out—there is no way to solve religious conflicts." Here, what is said is that to solve the question you have to look into the state itself—the structure of the state, the boundaries of the state. If you redraw the boundaries, this might contain the problems: create new autonomies and dismiss all this nonsense about sovereignty. Burn out these religious conflicts by redrawing religious boundaries—this is one way of looking at it.

MR. DENG: I was quite interested in what Mr. Laitin and also Mr. Gambari made of the balance of power in Nigeria in terms of one region having the political power, another region the economic power, and maybe even a third area having the bureaucratic power. The interesting thing is, as they hinted very correctly earlier, this is in distinction from the Sudan, because in the case of the Sudan all the deprivations are on one side, all the benefits on the other. The south is numerically in the minority, economically disadvantaged, and even religiously in the minority. Therefore, there is no way at all of bringing about a balance. What I find quite interesting here is the implication that Nigeria has found a kind of balance with which it is very comfortable. You do not see the northerners aspiring very conspicuously toward gaining economic power. You seem to indicate that southerners and easterners are quite content with their economic and bureaucratic power and are not that keen on seizing the political power. How stable is this in the long run?

MR. LAITIN: There is a difference between being content and wanting to destroy the state because you are discontent.

MR. GAMBARI: It is a tentative, very uneasy balance.

MR. DENG: As to the external situation, a point that Mr. Omer Beshir has underscored but that needs to be stressed: Have we lost the power to solve our problems within our own national boundaries because of these external factors, and does one then say, "Let us involve anybody who has any role at all"—is that practical? Or do we work to discard them and solve the problems within the boundaries?

Now, the interesting thing also is this question: Can religion play a role in solving problems? This brings me to this question of discourse. All the Sudanese, even the very scholarly, academically oriented people who would normally invite discussions, would seem to assume that [Dr. Hasan] Turabi cannot be talked to—he is a fundamentalist! I have seen many enlightened northern leaders who are secularists not even wanting to see Turabi. Whereas when you see Turabi you are fascinated by his reasoning and by the degree of what seems like flexibility if only the other side would come to him. The question really is: Is there really meaningful discourse going on or are we complaining in isolation?

The question of leadership in the Sudan going to a Christian is a very good one. I would recommend it very strongly . . . [Laughter] There was a vice-president from the south [about] whom everybody agreed that if he had run in the elections with Nimeiri he would have won, but because he was a southerner . . . He was vice-president over and over again while first vice-presidents came and went. I myself was minister of state for many years, and I saw many ministers come and go. There were times when Nimeiri would tell me before the reshuffle to get prepared for the task of becoming *the* minister of foreign affairs, and then when the announcement came I retained my position as minister of state. Although I do not mean to say that it had nothing to do with qualification . . . [Laughter] I was told by many people that Nimeiri could not take the idea of a southerner, a Christian, going to the Arab world and Islamic conferences as *the* minister of foreign affairs of the Sudan, and being minister of state I could do the job while somebody else represented the Sudan.

MR. GAMBARI: Let me add for the purpose of comparison that although I did not realize it, I was the first and probably the only Muslim who was foreign minister of Nigeria since independence. It is the opposite in Nigeria, it is the Christians that have been foreign ministers since independence.

MR. JOHNSON: It is interesting that the discussion moved in that direction this afternoon—toward clarifying, a finer teasing out of a number of assumptions we have been making this morning, even indeed up to the afternoon's opening speeches, which have now been clarified in some finer detail.

Just very briefly, there has been this overriding, what I would call deficit-model approach toward religion. By and large, in all the discussions thus far it has always been articulated in terms of "fire alarms" going off. The question has now been raised whether, in fact, we ought to have emphasized so exclusively the deficit-model analysis of religious activity. This has been opened up somewhat. I know the title of the symposium is Religion and *National* Integration in Africa, but one of my notes here is the question: To what extent can one separate national integration from its international dimension? Rather, very significantly, it has been brought up in terms of the internationalization of the kinds of issues that we have been raising.

Mr. Deng raised a question as to whether perhaps in Africa we have lost control of so much of our own context as to be unable to solve our problems. A partial response to that might be that there is something incongruous between the articulation of the view that Islam and Christianity are "world religions" and then not to expect such "world religions" to, by definition, bring in, for better or worse, a larger constituency. In this case, it might be very interesting to watch, as we all probably have done, the way in which Biafra's Christianity was internationalized during the Nigerian civil war. It seems to me that to tap into Islam as a world religion and to tap into Christianity as a world religion is by definition to tap into all of the international implications—good, bad, and indifferent—of that particular dimension.

We have also talked in terms of sects and about divisions of these categories of religions into sects. I was partly pleased, partly disturbed, by the way in which certain kinds of developments—take, for example, Christianity—were sort of put together as if they were straight-line developments. I am not sure that Aladura and what that phenomenon represents can be articulated in the same way as purely a sect, in the manner of Catholicism or Methodism. It seems to me something fundamentally different is going on there in terms of class formation, in terms of gender formation, et cetera. By and large, we have been talking about religion and religious activities in ways that, it seems to me, elide for a moment the question of gender formation. I think we have been developing categories of civil society, categories of governments, categories of public activity, that essentially privilege males and male roles. I am wondering, for example, if we break it down, whether the rate of conversion to these various sects of the various denominations are in terms of gender. Which gender enters much more quickly or less quickly into political society or into civil society or into the negotiation for power? Is it possible that in terms of certain kinds of newer movements developing in the urban areas in Nigeria and Sierra Leone you will tend to have demographically proportionately greater numbers of women between the ages of forty-five and fifty-five being "converted"? What are the implications for the demographic and gender formation of the particular kind of mass that we are talking about—whether in terms of the fact that we have men specifically in there or whether we have women in there? Or if we do not have enough women in these kinds of constructions, what are the implications for power formations or for the evolution of that area?

A final issue I wish to raise, which is ultimately my major point, is that although the discussion has invoked three categories of religion in Africa, I have been really quite struck by the fact that we have discussed with enormous fluency the Islamic dimension and the Christian dimension. The interesting part is that with virtually every speaker who has spoken thus far, I have noticed that the third dimension is always preceded either with a cough or with an apology. That is, it has always been something like, "There is Islam, there is Christianity, and then [coughs] traditional religion or so-called paganism or so-called custom, et cetera." [Laughter] Now, what are the implications of this? I am curious as to whether national integration or national consciousness or patterns of cognition or of language have some significant role to play in those particular areas? Is it likely, for example, that at election time in Yorubaland the Ifa oracle plays a far greater role in terms of national integration than Christianity or Islam? This we have really not discussed, and it seems to me rather critical. It may be at some point useful not to merely cough or apologize anthropologically when we talk about this other thing.

MR. DEMOZ: What has come up repeatedly, I think, is the fact that religion is part of a complex structure, a complex set of factors of identity that in some cases overlaps. The two cases we dealt with, the Sudanese one and the Nigerian one, provide an interesting contrast in this respect, because I think that what we have in Nigeria is a situation where they do cross-cut and sort of nullify each other's effect, while in the Sudan, although this has not been said explicitly, they seem to fall on top of each other and do help to explain at least some of the aspects of the intractability of the Sudanese case.

A country nearby that provides an interesting contrast, also about which nothing has been said, is Ethiopia, where we have all the same factors, except there too they do cross-cut—they do not fall on top of each other. Specifically I am speaking of language, territorial aggregation, and perhaps the state of economic development. I will speak about Ethiopia because I know it far better than I know the situation in Nigeria, although I think they are similar. In the case of Ethiopia, neither Islam nor Christianity is really territorially aggregated. Both tend to be spread, especially Islam, in little clumps all over the country. More importantly, neither Islam nor Christianity is coterminous with a language group. Christianity is practiced by several major language groups: Tigrean speakers, Amharic speakers, and many others I could name. Similarly with Islam. So you do not have this self-intensifying factor there either. There is no sense in which you could say that economically the Christians as a whole are more advantaged or the Muslims are less advantaged.

Because of this in Ethiopia, despite the tremendous fragmentation that it is now experiencing, none of that has been done around religion as a rallying point. Religion has been conspicuous by its absence in the Ethiopian fragmentation. Perhaps it is somewhat in the background in the Eritrean case, but very much in the background. Whereas in the Sudan we have the territorial aggregation largely between the south and the north—although there are some exceptions to this, I am sure—and we have the fact that Islam is largely coterminous with speakers of Arabic. Since language is one of the most important definers of ethnicity, when you have religion on top of that, and territorial aggregation on top of that, the tendency is for the cleavage to be far stronger than it would be if these were not coterminous with each other.

Now, what lessons can we draw from this? At least from an academic point of view, I think this strongly argues for a highly interdisciplinary approach to the question of integration. Rather than speaking about religion and national integration we perhaps ought to speak about language and religion and territorial aggregation and national integration, which is rather awkward and very long [Laughter], but I think we are resourceful enough to find some appropriate abbreviation for it. We really have to pull together whoever can look at the question from all these different perspectives and see why things are the way they are and what may be the way out of this grave difficulty.

I am also interested in what Mr. Omer Beshir said concerning the question of whether the issue can really be solved within the one-state framework, because this does relate to the fact that each of those religions in our part of the world does very much cut across state lines, as do indeed languages cut across state lines. But from a practical political point of view, it is of course much more difficult to bring any kind of agreement across state lines than within. Nevertheless, it is something which we should not consider impossible.

MR. AN-NA'IM: It seems to me that what Mr. Gambari was saying this morning about the historical compromise in Nigeria may not be as historical or as compromised in the sense that historically you did have those tensions and conflicts and that the compromise is not working as well or seems to be flagging already. What seems to be at issue here is that when you have Muslims and non-Muslims (whatever their sense of identification may be) who have lost political independence for a long time and then have regained that independence, within a short time they will start thinking in terms of self-determination for their particular religious identity or other type of identity. So what seems to be the case in Nigeria as in the Sudan is that—although I would not of course deny the economic and the social dimensions of the issue—it just takes some time for the issue to be cast in terms of self-determination for Muslims and a stronger association with Islamic identity, including the application of Sharia.

In this respect, I would like to disagree with Mr. Hunwick that it is not a question of what *type* of Sharia, but of what *degree* of Sharia you implement. What you indicate in terms of Nigeria, which is also true in the Sudan, is that Sharia has always been the personal law of Muslims. Now, the question comes when you go to the next stage, of reintroducing Sharia into the public sphere, in public law. There are of course differences of interpretation and so on, but the difference in the Sudan and Nigeria is not a difference of what type of Sharia, but what *degree* of application of Sharia. The allusion to Muslim secession in Nigeria in the event of a non-Muslim becoming head of state is of course a manifestation of Sharia, as you know. That is, from a Sharia point of view, Muslims are not supposed to be ruled by a non-Muslim. In fact, a non-Muslim should not exercise authority over non-Muslims. So this sentiment, though muted now and though we take it with a grain of salt, is indicative, I think, of an underlying current of a stronger association with Islamic identity.

Now, I would like to refer to Mr. Laitin's point that one cannot say society is more tolerant or less tolerant, but rather tolerant in relation to various aspect of society. I think this is very true. What seems to be the purpose of my exercise, and I am sure of most of you here, is to make societies tolerant in respect to those aspects that are most conducive to national integration—and if societies need to be *in*tolerant, to be intolerant in ways that will not repudiate these basic understandings. In other words, the link between religion and national integration from my perspective is a promotion of tolerance of those aspects that will further national integration and suppress tendencies toward disintegration.

Finally, in response to Mr. Beshir's point that religion has had a role in crisis creation or conflict creation but that it is possible that it may not have a role in conflict resolution, I would say that, to start with, we do not have a choice. That is, it is not as if we can start with no religion in the formula. Religion is already a part, a very integral part, of the complex situation itself. So it is a situation where we have to deal with religion: we have no choice in that respect. To the extent that religion is part of the issue it has to be dealt with as such. It is not simply a question of overlooking religion. We cannot afford to because it is part of the situation. In this respect, I would rather suggest that we work with religion, which is an integral part of the situation, and develop those aspects that make for tolerance in the significant way I have indicated.

MR. HUNWICK: In short, religion is not just going to go away. [Laughter] Some questions or comments from the floor . . . ?

FROM THE FLOOR: Concerning Mr. Gambari's point that if religious disagreements continue to be within a particular religion and do not spread to become one religion against another as they did in March 1987, there may not be another civil war, but if it happens again we may be in for some trouble in the future; and then his comment that there are some Nigerians studying in Saudi Arabia, there are some Nigerians now studying in Iran, and that they are coming back. I would like to ask him what he thinks about the future in terms of a major religious crisis that may be perpetuated in one way or another by outside influences, either by Nigerian citizens who are coming back from different parts of the world where Islam has different interpretations, or otherwise; whether that kind of conflict would come from the outside; or whether, if Nigeria disintegrates through a religious conflict, it will come from within?

FROM THE FLOOR: Mine is just a comment. Christian southerners in the Sudan never forget that the northern Sudan was at one time a Christian kingdom. Northern Sudanese think that Islam was the only power in the Sudan and that Christianity is something new, forgetting the fact that there *was* a Christian kingdom there that actually contributed to the Sudan culturally and has actually become part of the character and identity of the Sudan. So is this a problem of Christianity and Islam, [or] is this not really a political problem rather than a religious problem? Christianity and Islam are used for political gains by a few in the Sudan who are dominating the scene. The majority of the Sudanese unfortuately are not educated enough to realize the differences between them.

MR. GAMBARI: What I am trying to say is that as of now the religious riots in Nigeria are not strong enough by themselves to cause the country to go into another civil war, but that we should not be complacent about the situation at all. We should strengthen those who are committed to maintaining the secularity of the state. This would be a function of addressing some of the socioeconomic issues *within* regions in Nigeria and *between* regions in Nigeria. My fear is that with the return of these people trained in Iran, the increasing radicalization of youth, particularly in the northern universities, and the army of unemployed people . . . if the religious dimension then makes the interethnic, interregional situation worse and you have a north-south division, that is what can threaten the stability of Nigeria.

Religion, Politics, and National Integration: A Comparative African Perspective   LAMIN SANNEH

Western political thought, particularly since Machiavelli and Bodin, has assumed an absolute autonomy for political institutions, to be judged by independent criteria and with the nation-state as their supreme embodiment. Western political thought, however, was not confined to Western society but penetrated societies in Africa, Asia, South America, and elsewhere, as Sir Ernest Barker observed with reference to India.[1] Thus we in Africa, too, have become offshoots of the Western political heritage, even though our roots lie in a different soil. But precisely because of our relatively recent assimilation, we feel constrained to take a fresh look at inherited political institutions and ideas, a process of reappraisal in which Muslims have eagerly joined. I propose to do two things in this short presentation. I would like to suggest, first, that the sovereign state is not the absolute, all-sufficient instrument its defenders claim it is and, second and more importantly, that much religious thought lies at the source of the secular state. Under each of these interrelated themes I shall suggest something about the issue of national integration. Clearly, the state regards national integration as an overriding goal, whereas in terms of religious loyalty it is but a by-product of a larger, transcendent loyalty. The religious factor is thus critical to a reappraisal of the political issue, and for that reason we need to determine its place in the scheme of things. My basic assumption is that the recovery of some of this religious thought is a precondition for the revitalization of contemporary social and political life. What Christians and Muslims have to say on this matter, separately and together, needs to be included in any reasonable account of the modern ferment.

It seems to me that two major areas of concern have emerged from the impact of the secular state. One is the insufficiency of national, racial, or ethnic identity as a justification for the existence or function of the state, because national sovereignty alone is incapable of coping with the demands of a complex political, economic, and military order. Hence the significance of coalitions, alliances, and pacts between and across nations and the need for structures for international arbitration. The other is the precise role that religion plays in contemporary life, with religious questions often having ramifications that extend far beyond the jurisdiction of the state.

The evolution of the secular state from its origins in the eighteenth century has followed a path of articulate opposition to religion, fueled by the fundamental assumption that human life is lived in two different spheres, the public and the private; that the public sphere is superior in will to the private; and that the state is in absolute command of the public sphere. This view brings the state into potential conflict with persons whose conscience may lead them to decline the authority of the state. The self-confident claims of (and for) the state represent in this sense a corresponding downgrading of both the private sphere and the religious structures charged with its maintenance.

My thesis in this presentation may be simply stated thus: If we concede the absolutist claims of the secular state, then we have challenged the right of religion to make absolute claims for God. It may be put another way: If you absolutize the secular you must necessarily relativize the religious. By proceeding on one front, you must in fact proceed against the other, much in the manner of the traditional square dance: moving three steps to the left anticipates as many to the right. I need not belabor the point that the absolutized state incurs a double jeopardy: it cripples the instrumental function of authority and infects all of religious motivation with hypocrisy. Such a state demands absolute submission from its citizens; yet when people's temporal interests preclude that kind of absolute obligation, the goal of national integration is hindered.

Perhaps it could not have been foreseen, but the theory of political sovereignty in its fully developed sense created the atmosphere for the absolutization of political norms. For example, Marsiglio of Padua, a medieval writer who straddled the Middle Ages and early modern Europe, "asserted the primacy of law-making over all other expressions of state power; he insisted on the indivisibility of ultimate legislative authority."[2] Although Marsiglio did not develop his ideas into a coherent theory of sovereignty, by stressing the formal right of the ruler to make laws he provided grist for the mill of theoreticians. Two important elements characterize medieval writings about political authority: the first is the role assigned to reason and natural law, and the second is the emphasis placed on political obligation, with little concern for how some forms of political behavior could be accepted as alternatives to obedience. The ruler is assumed to be beholden to norms of reason and justice, but in fact the circularity of thought involved makes those norms themselves attributes of the ruler. What you give with the right hand you take with the left.

There are many reasons why politics and religion are interlinked, but nothing better illustrates their problematic relationship than the issue of authority. We have inherited from medieval political thought a formidable problem of the nature and limits of political obligation, of how human beings may give due recognition to the right of the state to command their loyalty while retaining the inalienable right to recognize no higher authority than God. How the state can make ultimate claims on our loyalty and not come into conflict with our ultimate right to recognize no higher law than God inflames much of the anxiety today.

Perhaps one way of saying this is to argue that the secular state as presently constituted has reached the limits of its development and that henceforth our task is to define those limits, whether in terms of basic human rights or the new international order.

Indeed, I would argue that the current religious ferment is a reflection of this situation, with religious people determined to demonstrate their version of the limited applicability of political sovereignty. The widespread phenomenon of citizens confronting their governments and challenging policies in both the public and private spheres shows a remarkable awakening of popular distrust vis-à-vis the omnipotent state.

The secular liberal prescription of the activist, welfare state, so strong in the generation since the end of World War II, has been abandoned in the face of disenchantment. Yet the theoretical underpinnings for the state as both means and end have remained firmly in place. That fact, plus the extended range of the modern state, has incited a countermovement among religious groups, in Africa and elsewhere.

We have assumed that the state is a rational institution and that as such it sets the bounds necessary for rational conduct in society. Beyond that we have ascribed to the state exclusive authority, which justifies rules of ethics and morality that obtain their coherence from the rational state. But despite such assumptions we find instances of people resisting the will of the state—and the more preponderant that will, the more implacable the resistance. Similarly, in the international arena claims for rights are pressed that, at least in theory, seriously qualify the sovereign status of states. When we have spoken of reform and renewal of public life and institutions, we have seldom included the idea of curtailing the power of the state itself.

Yet we can scarcely do otherwise. The secular state is not just the innocent victim of religious controversy; it is itself the perpetrator of that controversy, for by absolutizing itself it claims the power not just to organize life and command the obedience of men and women but to be itself what H. Richard Niebuhr calls "the value-center," consecrating the whole enterprise with a new form of faith: the henotheist faith of national loyalty.[3] It is a short step from this to saying that the state in fact is "the shadow of God on earth," followed by the third step of making obligation and loyalty matters exclusively of state control.

One response to this situation is to object that the state contravenes rational norms if men and women must behave toward it as if it were God's deputy. But that response is not original, for it borrows language—that is, discourse—steeped in the utilitarian premise, created by the state and in a form familiar to the state. Before moving beyond it, we should spell out the objection and thus show the ultimate inadequacy of the omnipotent state. Such a state arrogates to itself not only the power to restrain and arbitrate but also to prescribe faith of a certain kind and conformity of a certain pattern. Secular thinkers who might originally have opposed the idea of a corporate religious state where clerics and cardinals were also majors and magistrates would thus have inherited in this omnipotent state a new corporate will in the omniscient bureaucrat and ubiquitous police agent. Whereas before blasphemy might have been threatened with forgiveness averted, now it would be considered from the perspective of ultimate state interest. So complete would be the authority of the state that a special virtue might be inferred from the otherwise cynical view that if the state loses the confidence of the people, it should dissolve the people and elect another.

My basic contention here is not the facile romanticism of a stateless society where people revert to an exotic innocence, but that the omnipotent state is really its own undoing. This leads me to my next point: namely, an original religious position regarding the life of the state is that political instruments were fundamentally necessary to the maintenance of a just and decent society but that these instruments were not themselves the truth of God. To say, for example, that the state is of this world is to imply that its boundaries are limited relative to another sphere. Religious persons, being also social persons, participate simultaneously in the two spheres, the worldly and the religious. But the affinity of religious persons with the worldly is only an analogy, a metaphor, of their affinity with the spiritual. The material forms of existence particularize in their pluralism God's providence and sustenance, which compose our earthly and heavenly welfare. Religious persons relativize earthly arrangements by an act of faith invoking

God, the true absolute, thus creating the paradox of joining the two spheres even at the moment that they are being separated. In this sense, the separation of powers doctrine is not the exclusion of religion or politics from each other's sphere, but their relation to the compound theme of human existence and destiny, of historical contingency and moral truth. It is not primarily a question of the moral versus the immoral, of truth against falsehood, but of human participation in the One and the Many.

Consider for a moment what might be involved. If the issue were merely one of competing claims between religion and politics, each assumed to be autonomous absolute departments of life, then the solution to any conflict between them would be easy and simple, like separating the skins of an onion. Caesar would pursue his vocation steering a straight course out of the range of God, while the party of God could tend the Lord's vineyard during overtime. The picture, however, is more complex than that. Religion and politics are intimately connected: they affect each other, draw on each other's insight, are sustained from a common stock of human encounter and endeavor, and receive from people loyalty and affirmation as well as direction and purpose. Yet history and circumstance have forced a divergence between the two. Religion was perceived to exist in the private, voluntary sphere, a sort of tolerated enclave into which people drift when the main business of life was over, while politics pertained to the public, compulsory sphere, which constituted the truth center. The picture emerged that politics impinged on religion in a superior way, that if religion was prominent it was because it shone with the reflected light burning at the core of the sovereign state. The subtle interplay between the two became overlaid with the refracted light issuing from politics, with religion now glimpsed in the afterglow of state authority. The derivative character of religion was thus established. In other words, the church was a vestige of the superior and all-comprehending claim of the political state, an elaborate ritual screen without substance.

In the present ferment and turbulence, such a sanguine view of the all-purpose state cannot command our full assent. The

Islamic counterargument, now the topic in media and print reports, for example, is symptomatic of the widespread disenchantment with conventional wisdom concerning the state. The Islamic criticism is that the state has become a false absolute, an expression of *shirk*, even though standard Islamic prescriptions are not necessarily any more encouraging. But at least the issues are being hotly debated across the board. There is in fact no Christian case comparable to the Islamic situation. Even in the United States, where we have witnessed the resurgence of the conservative religious right, the anticlimactic careers of some of the chief protagonists suggest how ephemeral, if dramatically repetitive, the phenomenon can be. Why Islam appears to foster much more hospitable grounds for the setting of the religious agenda in public affairs deserves very careful consideration.

The traditional Islamic teaching that there is no distinction between religion and politics, the sacred and the secular, affirms, on one level of analysis, the interconnection between the two. There are obviously great areas of complexity, but we cannot in the case of Islam continue to apply the facile rule that the state commands the instruments of coercion to make its will effective in the public domain while religion looks to personal conscience for its teachings to be authoritative in the private sphere. We discover in the light of the Islamic comparison that even in democratic societies political parties are voluntary associations that, once in power, translate policies into laws that in turn are continually modified through the legislative process. Similarly, churches may command resources whose allocation and concentration create lines of power. Legislators themselves may differ over policy issues and still agree on the safeguard of noncoercion, while laws enacted may be considerably modified in the courts by arguments of humanity or whatever. Similarly, prelates may preside over ecclesiastical courts to enforce rules of discipline, family life, property, and a host of other matters. Canon law may not direct traffic, and parliamentary law may not decide the content of the communion cup, but that does not mean that the two spheres have nothing to do with each other. Thus, the Islamic position has a measure of validity. The secular state might find that its authority declined with decreasing use of the element of persuasion and, conversely, that its earthly life was enhanced by the public use of religious counsel; in short, matters of its earthly security may not be disconnected from matters of religious truth. Indeed, the true safeguard to political integrity is consent, not coercion, in the same way that religious wisdom might demand the functional separation of the two. Thus, politics and religion both require spiritual commitment for their authority to be effective: religious ideals must seek practical channels of human improvement to sustain faith, while political practice tends to build a tradition of loyalty that is at heart a spiritual value. They balance each other in a complementarity where one is not the parody of the other. The bridge between religion and politics is thick with reciprocal traffic, though the connection may become tenuous if maintained by formal gestures, postures we take up for show.

There is widespread apprehension here and elsewhere that religion by definition implies intolerance and that introducing it into politics makes for a virulent form of bigotry. Much of what has happened when religious leaders have assumed political power confirms this apprehension. In our day, however, the pluralist character of life requires a revaluation of the state as the remedy for religious intolerance and the answer for national integration.

The religious case for a functional separation of church and state should now be investigated. If on one level religion and politics are inseparable, on another they ought to be scrupulously kept apart. Even in the Islamic tradition there are forces arguing for such a separation. One classical Islamic source, for example, strives to make a distinction between the two realms, suggesting that worldly affairs should not be allowed to corrupt the things of religion. He puts it in the form of an epigrammatic statement, to wit, that the best of worldly rulers are those who visit the *'ulamā'* (religious scholars), and the worst of the *'ulamā'* are those who visit worldly rulers. Here the hazardous relation of politics and religion is recognized and a hint given of the religious interest in keeping them distinct. The two spheres, however closely related, are not equivalent or interchangeable. The standard formulation of *dār al-islām* and *dār al-ḥarb*, the realm of belief and that of unbelief, actually sets the stage for a similar distinction in religion and politics, whatever the correctness of the position regarding their inseparability. Unless *dār al-islām* exists for those who are there under coercion—which it clearly does not—its best safeguard lies in the absence of compulsion. In fact, the sacred Qur'an (2:256) affirms that there is no compulsion in religion (*lā ikrāha fi-d-dīn*). From the religious point of view, a prescriptive state would play into the hands of charlatans at one extreme and bigots at the other. Many people would choose to join or remain in the religious fold for eminently sound religious reasons, but many would also stay for very bad religious reasons—from fear of reprisal, hope of gain, or the force of blackmail—a situation that is fatal to the spiritual motive. Similarly, the prescriptive state would make it impossible to treat nonconformists, religious or other, with anything but cynical contempt.

In the discussions that have taken place about the contemporary need for a prescriptive Islamic state, much attention has been focused on non-Muslims, and in particular on minorities. Although some advocates have assured skeptics that such a state would have cast-iron guarantees enshrined in the constitution, many on both the Muslim and non-Muslim sides remain unconvinced. Privileges conferred on minority groups in a prescriptive state very soon carry the stigma of exclusion, with constitutional measures becoming inquisitional staging posts, society's handy valve for disgorging unassimilated elements in a time of crisis.

The great Ibn Khaldūn observed that the ideological mixing of religion and politics wreaks havoc on the moral foundations of religion. Political contingency, he argued, provides a dubious base for theological consistency, and actions taken in response to historical pressure should not be inflated with the sanction of principle. It is a matter of deep interest to religious persons that empirical reality be recognized for what it is rather than being predicated on the ideal realm. Ibn Khaldūn explored the social and historical situation in the belief that critical religious reflection might help us steer our way and offer a goal to make the effort worthwhile. He was not sanguine enough about the moral character of rulers to believe that we should trust them with being able to read correctly the signposts of history, let alone the invisible writing of the divine. A verse from the Qur'an (27:34) supports this distrust, speaking about how rulers, "when they enter a town, corrupt it, and make the upper classes of its people the meanest; so will they do." There is even a sense in which the transitoriness of human trophies serves as a lesson for placing earthly arrangements in their proper perspective; those who cling to these things without a moral sense are like persons who accumulate records. Such works "are like ashes upon which the wind blows strongly on a day of hurricane, they cannot keep hold of any of what they have piled up" (14:21).

In concluding this aspect of our treatment, it may be observed that the most fundamental restriction on the power of rulers in Islam is the primacy of the religious code, sometimes identified with reason (*'aql*). In theory, at least, the ruler is subject to the code and may not add to or take from it; thus rulership has an essentially executive rather than legislative function. A work composed in 1302 elaborates this view, pointing out how power is divided into two parts, the religious and the temporal.[4] Nizam al-Mulk, another medieval scholar—indeed, the Islamic Machiavelli—wrote on the theme, and in his case, too, considerations of *raison d'état* led him to exempt the ruler from observance of certain parts of the code.[5] Even the indefatigable al-Ghazali, writing much earlier than Ibn al-Tiqtaqa, made wide concessions for rulers, such being the nature of the near-absolute power they wielded.[6] Today the heirs to that tradition include Colonel Gadhafi of Libya, General Zia of Pakistan, and, of course, the Ayatollah Khomeini of Iran.

When we look to the Christian side, the case is at least as compelling. Many Christian leaders in this century have spoken about the importance of religious counsel in political and economic matters; many, perhaps a substantial proportion, are concerned about pragmatic and institutional safeguards for individual freedom and human rights in the modern state, convinced that there would be adequate room within such safeguards for the church to flourish. Some others—the vocal moral minority, if you will—argue for a central role for the church, afraid that its peripheral status has reduced its influence over practical affairs. Nevertheless, I think everyone concerned agrees that the days of Christian hegemony are over, and that even if Christian renewal were to come about, it would have to be in the context of a continuing pluralism in modern life. Yet it would be a mistake to think that pluralism is anything new. The Christians of the first centuries were plunged into a complex world of the Judaic heritage; Roman imperial politics, provincial life, and customs; social diversity; linguistic plurality; and the heady ferment of Greek intellectual achievement. Augustine argues in this pluralist context that rule should be not by naked will power, "the lust for domination," but by the office of counseling.[7]

The questions concerning the nature of state authority and the rights of individuals today press in on us from all sides, partly because in the non-Western world the state as a Western heritage seems inadequate for the tasks it faces: too big for the small problems and too small for the great problems. Christians in that part of the world often constitute only a small proportion of the populace, but their significance far outweighs their number—the logical contrary of the situation in the West, where statistical preponderance is met with religious marginalization. Third World Christians, therefore, bear a heavy responsibility for providing much needed input on the reappraisal of the state, and it seems no accident that in several African countries those national leaders who are prepared to question the adequacy of the modern state for African needs are self-declared Christians. That reappraisal has been considerably distorted by the vagaries of East-West ideological confrontation. The one overriding issue that fuels criticism—not to mention instability—of the modern state in Africa and elsewhere is the great pluralist heritage of the continent and the misfit of a state apparatus designed for homogeneity, for which "national integration" often acts as handy camouflage.

Since the modern state is founded on the ethos of linguistic unity, religious uniformity, and social conformity, its transplanting to Africa has exposed serious gaps in its operation. We are gravely handicapped in Africa for not having the critical tradition that accompanied the birth of the modern state in the West. Many ordinary people consequently feel that the state is an imposition, which they try to evade by withdrawal into their natural communities. One would like to be able to assure them that even in the West critical counsel went into shaping political thought and institutions.

For example, to show that religious thinkers were alert to historical contingency, Sir Thomas More wrote about the moral foundations of the new economics that was gaining ascendancy in his time. In his celebrated work *Utopia* he dealt with the reality of early-sixteenth-century England in an effort to check the excesses of prevailing economic forces. He did this by attempting to expose the defects of the emerging secular state, submitting it to the standards of the Sermon on the Mount. More's approach turned the two-ends doctrine around: that is, the worldly kingdom and the spiritual kingdom, he maintained, are not irrelevant to each other (an insight deepened by close reading of Augustine's *City of God*). More felt that God's claim on us should oblige us (or at any rate him) to establish a City of Man that God would not disdain to dwell in—which means securing it on the foundations of its heavenly prototype.

With an ambiguous legacy of political involvement and withdrawal, the church came to find itself lurching toward an increasingly self-confident state and winding down to a subservient position. The view became respectable that the church should yield political authority to the state, including the definition of what authority should be. Thus was the Erastian state conceived. Yet neither the state nor the church was content with such a redrawing of the boundaries, for if a pious ruler could be trusted to observe the distinction, an ambitious worldly-minded prince would likely run cart and horse through the arrangement.

It was with Richard Hooker (1554–1600) that the first ambitious attempt was made to define the ecclesiastical polity (the title of his influential work) in such a way that the national state may be entrusted with its safety. Hooker was a religious radical but a theological moderate. He accepted the rational law, or the light of reason or nature, as no less authoritative than divine injunction, but he rejected the antinomian strains of Puritan thought with its relentless anti-Catholic tendencies. Hooker would have nothing to do with the Barthianism of the Puritans, the theology that set a God of inscrutable will "over against" the "accursed nature of Man." That dialectic creates an extremism of the "right" and the "left" at the same time: ask of any institution whether it is of God, in which case you fall down and worship, or whether it is of Man, then you attack and destroy it. Unlike the bulk of the Puritans, Hooker was not searching for the true church and could never have prayed with Donne, "Show me deare Christ, thy spouse."[8] Hooker's view of the relation between church and state, rather, was conditioned by his premise that Christianity is by its nature what Edward Gibbon would call "a religion of the provinces"—that is, a religion that assimilates into the characteristics of national cultures.[9] This pluralism was important to Hooker's thesis about the church including those who might be excluded from the "sound" part of the church as heretics, idolaters, and other wicked persons, and about the church belonging equally to the two realms of this world and the next. Hooker believed that the churches are "rather like diverse families than like divers [*sic*] servants of one family," so that no "one certain form" of polity need be common to them all.[10]

Hooker's notion of ecclesiastical government is connected to his doctrine of political power. The church has the power to make laws to govern herself—but the church defined according to Hooker's understanding is a pretty inclusive body. Similarly, the realm over which the prince presides is a pretty inclusive community where everyone, including the prince, is under the law. Therefore, the prince may be seen as head of the church *intra ecclesiam non supre ecclesiam*, exercising "dominion" in ecclesiastical matters according to the laws of the church. For Hooker, "sovereignty" lies only in one source: heaven. Yet the nation-church that came into being under Hooker's scheme did pretend to possess sovereignty to coerce Nonconformists, recusants, and Puritans. Furthermore, had not Hooker laid the groundwork for "Anglicanism" as a universal idea that sanctioned and accompanied the expansion of England abroad? Merely to argue, as Hooker did, that his critics had not promulgated a dispensation that did not itself coerce is scarcely sufficient to resolve the problems he inherited with his premises. Perhaps it would be best to augment Hooker with Henry Venn (d. 1873), the great architect of missions under Anglicanism, for it was he who insisted that the goal of missions was the establishment of national churches, not the perpetuation of Church of England ecclesiastical protectorates.[11] That approach helped to preserve religious pluralism within the church.

All ages have their shibboleths, powerful generalizations that exert an influence beneath the surface of thought. Our age is marked by a shibboleth every bit as pervasive as those of previous ages. The general assumptions about church and state being separate belong to this category, making it extremely difficult to mobilize opinion in a different direction. In his book *The Coming World Civilization*, the American philosopher William Ernest Hocking expounds what has come to stand as the great shibboleth of our age. "We rely," he writes, "on the political community to do its part in the making of men, but first of all to furnish the conditions under which men can make themselves." A swift, and perhaps un-thought-out, transition follows at this point, according to Hocking. "The state, purely as secular, comes to be regarded as capable of civilizing the human being, and in doing so, of remaking him, training his will, moralizing him." Yet the political community as the repository of "memory and of hope" is not sufficient to play back to us those qualities through which our impulses and instincts can mature fully. Something else is needed.

Human nature has indeed another mirror, and there with another source of self-training. It has often the religious community—let us call it in all its forms "the church"—which has promised to give the human individual the most complete view of his destiny and of himself. It projects that destiny beyond the range of human history. . . . It provides standards of self-judgment not alone in terms of behavior, as does the law, but also in terms of motive and principle of the inner man which the state cannot reach.

The salient bias of the contemporary world, Hocking alleges, is how

the secular state tends to regard itself as the more reliable interpreter of human nature—dealing as it does solely with verifiable experience—and as a sufficient interpreter. . . . Outside the Marxist orbit, the prevalent disposition of the secular state in recent years has been less to combat the church than to carry on a slow empirical demonstration of the state's full equivalence in picturing the attainable good life, and its superior pertinence to actual issues. As this demonstration gains force the expectation grows that it will be the church, not the state, that will wither away.[12]

It is, I believe, in the Third World that this ideological core of the secular state has expanded enormously, seeing "the church," in Hocking's definition, along with other symbols of pluralism as barriers in its path. In many places in Africa people have responded with passive resistance, which the state has sought to overcome by arguing for national integration, justifying self-serving projects of mind and might by that argument. Such a state has set itself on a collision course with its people, whom it blames for opposing its provocative policies. Political rhetoric in Africa seeks to compensate for the actual contraction of the power base of the state, with development projects being used as brokerage in dealings with an unwilling citizenry. All this suggests that national integration must precede state effectiveness rather than merely follow it. Africa's pluralist heritage is far too indelibly inscribed in the souls of its peoples to capitulate at the whim of a doctrinaire state. As the anonymous wise man of the old dispensation in Africa put it in the Akan tongue, *Aban wo twuw n'dazi; wo nnsua no:* "Governments, too often heavily weighted with power, are to be pulled along the ground but not to be carried."[13]

Notes

1 Ernest Barker, *Principles of Social and Political Theory* (Oxford: Clarendon Press, 1951), vi.

2 Ewart Lewis, *Medieval Political Ideas* (New York: Cooper Square, 1974), 1:30.

3 See H. Richard Niebuhr, *Radical Monotheism and Western Culture* (New York: Harper & Bros., 1960).

4 Muhammad b. 'Alī ibn al-Ṭiqṭaqā, *al-Fakhrī*, trans. C.E.J. Whitting (London: Luzac, 1947), 14ff.

5 Niẓām al-Mulk, *The Book of Government or Rules for Kings* (London: Routledge and Kegan Paul, 1978).

6 Abū Hāmid al-Ghazālī, *The Book of Counsels for Kings* (London: Oxford University Press for Durham University, 1964).

7 Augustine, *City of God*, trans. Henry Bettenson (Harmondsworth, Eng.: Penguin Books, 1972), 19.15 (p. 875).

8 Cited in C. S. Lewis, "English Literature in the Sixteenth Century," in *The Oxford History of English Literature* (London: Oxford University Press, 1954), 454.

9 Gibbon develops this view in *Decline and Fall of the Roman Empire* (New York: Modern Library, n.d.), 1:418.

10 Lewis, "English Literature," 455.

11 Max Warren (ed.), *To Apply the Gospel: Selections from the Writings of Henry Venn* (Grand Rapids, Mich., 1971), 77–78. See also Wilbert Shenk, *Henry Venn: Missionary Statesman* (New York: Orbis Books, 1983).

12 William Ernest Hocking, *The Coming World Civilization* (London: George Allen & Unwin), 1958), 1–3.

13 F. L. Bartels, *The Roots of Ghana Methodism* (Accra: Methodist Book Depot; London: Cambridge University Press, 1965), 241–42.

Discussion of Lamin Sanneh's Paper

MR. GAMBARI: Two points interest me in what Mr. Sanneh has said. One is the question of the religious foundation of authority. When I reflect on that I ask the question: In the African context, in say the Nigerian or Sudanese context, whose religion are we talking about in terms of the religious foundation of authority? What foundation? Which authority? I am not simply asking Mr. Sanneh to respond, although I hope he might consider it worthwhile to do so. I am trying to clarify this in my own mind when I ask the question: Whose religion? If we are talking about the religious foundation of authority, whose religion are we talking about in a multireligious society? Christian? Muslim? and [coughs] traditional religion? [Laughter] Second, are we talking about the national foundation of a religiously based authority or a parochial foundation? Which one of these is possible in a plural society? Finally, which authority are we talking about? Secular authority? Then how do you go about laying the religious foundation of secular authority? Perhaps even more seriously, if you are talking about religious authority, to say that you have a religious foundation of religious authority would seem to me very tautological.

So in thinking about some of these very philosophical issues that Mr. Sanneh has raised, I feel that someone like myself who operates at the level of theory and practice has to have much more modest conceptions, and first that would be to reflect on the basis for the coexistence of faiths and religious tolerance in our various countries. Second, how to employ religion to strengthen the moral fiber of modern national societies? In other words, the use of religion to strengthen the authority of the family as a moral instrument for dealing with the growing urban social crises.

Now, these are very practical questions which I have been addressing perhaps from a philosophical starting point. I then can only come to the conslusion that perhaps what is of practical concern to someone like myself is the foundation of national political leadership and political authority which uses the best that religion can offer without being consumed by the divisions of religion, particularly the divisiveness of religion in a plural society, and how to build legitimacy of national political leadership and authority based on the fulfillment of the collective aspiration of the people. These are the practical issues I have distilled from the philosophical exposition that Mr. Sanneh has given. Particularly the issue of the religious foundation of authority is a very important one.

Finally, concerning the concluding remarks about the omnipotent state in Africa. I wonder which state is actually omnipotent in Africa? The pretense may be there, but the reality is not omnipotence, but impotence. That is why in most countries in Africa the state as embodied in the central authority is so fragile. You hear an announcement on the radio that there has been a military coup or change of government and most people in many countries of Africa will just shrug. So the government in Lagos or Accra has changed, so what? The link between the central authority and the majority of the people is *so* tenuous. I do not see omnipotence at all. I see a very patchy exercising of authority, which sometimes does not go beyond the capital. Not omnipotence. Perhaps we even have to strengthen the central authorities in plural societies and discover how to build legitimacy. Those are the reactions which this philosophic exposition of Mr. Sanneh has engendered in a practical man like myself.

MR. DENG: My initial reaction to the paper was that it should be a last word, not open to discussion. But one comment I have is that it really has underscored what I think is the weakest point in our discussion of so-called fundamentalists. That is to say, they have succeeded in capturing the moral high ground. They are defending religion and all that is morally right while we argue against God and all the ideals that God symbolizes. They seem to be the ones arguing for God and all the values associated with that.

On a personal note, I come from a part of the Sudan and from a family that really brings together all these things we are talking about. We had a father who was not a Muslim but who always entertained a *feki* in his home praying for him and a Dinka traditional religious expert performing the same function. I start-ed as a traditional Dinkaland believer, went to a Catholic school, proceeded to a Protestant school, went to a Muslim school, went to Khartoum University, got confused in the process . . . [Laughter] But I tried to assimilate all of this. When I am talking to very religious people I speak of having been enriched from the spiritual point of view by all these experiences. Just a few years ago I was involved in a very complex mediation process in the Sudan which went on for some months. Now, I had an elderly uncle and my mother sometimes staying up all night praying, and when I would go to the negotiations they would go through the rituals of blessing my tongue so that I would say the right thing in the process of negotiations. They were traditional people who had never been to any schools and had not been Catholics or Protestants. I took them very seriously. At every ritual they performed I felt that their care was a communication of something very profound and important. I really felt that I was uplifted by those rituals in going to those discussions. Which is to say all of these religions are really all there in one.

I want all of this to lead to one practical question: What do we *do*? Building on the kind of analyses and classic perceptions of these problems, how do we apply that to solve these problems that we have in countries like the Sudan and Nigeria? What policy implications and practical lines of action do we derive from this analysis?

DISCUSSION

MR. BESHIR: My comment would be that having lived all my life, really, in the Sudan and seeing the change in the last fifteen years—living the crisis daily, discussing it in small circles, now discussing it in a wider circle and coming here—I say let us stop analysis, we have had enough analysis. I do not want to be misunderstood. We welcome new analysis, but we have only been talking and analyzing. We are not *doing*. What should we *do*? We are always dissecting things, diagnosing things, knowing things. Those of us who live in the situation have different perceptions and priorities from those who do not live within the community itself. In every meeting I attend now, especially with the younger generation, they say: "Hey, we have a real problem. We are falling apart. People are dying! Where do we go from here? We cannot afford to continue like this!" So my comment is that we need to give a bit of thought to what *action* is needed. I think we cannot afford to go on just talking. We have to take some action. The fundamentalist has taken action. He is not analyzing. He is organized, so we need a concrete program for action.

MR. DEMOZ: I wonder if it might be useful to make a distinction between Religion with a capital *R* and religion with a lower case *r*. When we speak of secularization or "secular fundamentalism" we are certainly not talking about excluding Religion with a capital *R*. Indeed, there is a big question as to whether it can be excluded at all. It is so much a part of the life of African states and peoples. In the West as well, I do not think secularization has ever come in the form of excluding fundamental values, religious values. They have found their way into the polity through some other means, through concepts of natural law, throught the Bill of Rights, and many other ways. I think the question at issue is, should we really make the awesome coercive power of the state accessible to *specific* religions? Those who answer no to that are arguing for secularization. This is my understanding.

FROM THE FLOOR: Are we not really overemphasizing the role of religion? I think that this is not really the basic issue. The fundamental issue is the socioeconomic injustices, which more or less have to do with the access of the popular masses to resources. These have produced frustrations that manifest themselves in these religious movements.

MR. SANNEH: As a broad comment, it is part of my understanding of pluralism that I hope we can take inputs from different levels of reflection and analysis and that those who have more experience at practical affairs will make their contribution to the subject and those of us who have not had that privilege and are much more involved at the academic level can also make our contribution. But beyond that I would say there is, I think, enormous value in challenging people from across different religious lines to concentrate their minds on this question and bring their own contribution. Hopefully, something useful and valuable will emerge.

I really honestly think we are naive if we believe that we can force a separation between religion and politics. A recent *New York Times* report about President Botha in South Africa was for me a vivid reminder of how political leaders, secular leaders, will want to invoke moral and religious criteria to legitimate their authority and their policies. And they *will* do it badly because in a sense what they are doing is absolutizing the relative instrument of politics. They are using moral arguments to make absolute and final for themselves values that they hold as political leaders.

A few months ago I read a paper by Caspar Weinberger when he was still defense secretary of the United States in which he was talking about Star Wars [the Strategic Defense Initiative]. The article, published in a journal of Tufts University, is absolutely steeped in moral and religious language—absolutely steeped. Star Wars had begun to take on the dimensions of a religious issue, and all his language was steeped in moral discourse. Well, you are not going to be able to respond to him unless you know, you understand, what is going on there. There is an absolutization of the political process itself, and that is deeply harmful, is deeply corrupting to politics, let alone religion. You may want to defend religion, but it is more important, more immediately important, that we defend politics as really the realm of penultimate values, not the realm of the ultimate, because if you do that then you have a problem with what you do with the dissenters in the society. Those dissenters, in Caspar Weinberger's language, are actually rebels against God. They are rebels in the fundamental, ultimate sense of the word. That is terrible for a pluralist society. So I think we are naive if we think we can make that separation.

So what are the religious foundations of political authority? It begins with the assertion that the state is a human instrument that exists for our use and for our benefit; that there is nothing eternal or sacrosanct or absolute about the state; that we can change it—*must* change it—when it suits us, when it does not satisfy our needs we have a right to change it; that there is nothing absolute or eternal or sacrosanct about it. This is a religious principle. Second, the religious view says—and it really is a derivative of this first premise—that all human arrangements are by their very nature relative, and because they are relative they are plural. Therefore, of all these other arrangements that we see around us, no *one* arrangement excludes another. No one secular maneuver is inherently superior to another. The only reason we settle on certain maneuvers is because they happen to be more conducive to our welfare, to our interests, than others.

Therefore, we have a religious obligation from the religious point of view to advance intellectual arguments that would make pluralism respectable. One of the great problems in Africa is that we see pluralism as an obstacle to be overcome, as a problem. So we see ethnicity or tribal particularity or linguistic pluralism or religious pluralism as obstacles. Now . . . how do we talk about it? We talk about it in religious terms. We allocate to the state religious vocabulary to confront this diversity in our society. So we say the state transcends ethnic value. Now, transcendence is a religious value. If we believe it really belongs to the secular and the political domain, we are corrupting the instruments of politics. The state does not transcend anything or anybody. It only exists for our convenience.

It seems to me that contributions that we can make to the whole discussion should help to facilitate the idea that if the state is a human instrument, then religion itself has an instrumentality right at its very heart. Our Muslim friends who may be arguing for a religious state should be pressed to see that, ultimately, if they get to the point where instead of raising the *takbīr*, "Allāhu akbar," Muslims are saying "Islāmu akbar," the point they will have reached will be a corruption of Islam. Here the *takbīr* is no longer to God, rather it is to Islam. This is a corruption. It is not *takbīr*, it is *takabbur*—pride. Such is the very source of religious corruption and hypocrisy.

So we have an interest in religious systems themselves as being highly relative and plural in their very nature. When we talk about complexities, Mr. Beshir has mentioned the complexities within religious groups and religious associations. I take that very seriously. I say that complexity you are talking about is a reminder to me that my form of religion, my understanding of religion is not absolute and exclusive and normative for how God works in the world. If I do not believe that, then obviously I have made a fetish of my particular religious denomination.

In reference to Mr. Gambari's point about the omnipotent state, I think we misunderstand each other. We are saying really basically the same thing. What I am referring to is the *doctrine* of state omnipotence. That is to say, the *rhetoric* of state omnipotence becomes inflated at the moment when the state authority itself is in shambles. This rhetoric—"The *state* transcends our differences; the *state* interests require such and such; this person is a danger to the *state*"—is mobilized against certain kinds of enemies. In the meantime, the state is using coercion in a very nonproductive way because it is inflamed by the ideology of omnicompetence, which contends that the state can do it all, can see it all, can be it all. That is a lie. It is no more true in Africa than anywhere else. So Mr. Gambari and I are indeed talking about the same thing.

Returning to national leadership and political leadership, yes, I think that leadership must see itself almost in religious terms. There is a mission today that the national leadership, political leadership in Africa, must undertake on behalf of Africa. The very fact that our political leaders see their positions as a means toward wealth, to make money, is a corruption of the very values they are pretending to defend with political authority. At the end of the day those same rulers with all of their wealth are not going to have a society in which to enjoy their wealth. So, it is not working. We need a missionary, if you like, obligation to regard leadership as stewardship. This is really going back to the Islamic concept of the *khilāfa*. The *khalīfa* [caliph] is the steward of God on earth who takes responsibility for the wealth of this world on behalf of a God to whom the leader will have to give an account. You may say this is rather too idealistic and abstract and mystical, but believe me, it is the only way to secure the benefits of our material resources for our people. We need to have a sense of higher obligation—that the power we possess, the wealth we possess as stewards, is to be undertaken for the benefit of our people.

Finally, a point about religion and religions. I am not afraid of pluralism; I *am* a little bit afraid of religion as a kind of universal law. For me that undercuts the human phenomenon that is there in all of this, and therefore you must have pluralism. One of the great intellectual crises we face in the modern West is our inability to cope with pluralism. It is a fact of life! When I was in Britain and I went to Wales on holiday, when I went to the bank or a shop, the people there were speaking Welsh as a matter of pride. Living in Scotland I saw immediately that people were protesting against the dominance of central government. In our discourse in the West we are so controlled by the idea of the state as a unitary instrument against which we do all

of our sociology, political science, and the like that we are
unable to cope with pluralism. In Africa this has had disastrous
consequences for our people. Political renewal in Africa must
begin with curtailing the power of the state.

MR. KABA: Mr. Sanneh, I may have misunderstood you and would
like you to clarify two issues for me. By referring to the state as a
human creation, I am just wondering what do you think then
of religion? You know, I am sure, the work of Clifford Geertz,
who contends that religion is a cultural phenomenon. How do
you reconcile these two? Second, I would like you to elaborate a
reference you made that perhaps I misunderstood. You said that
in many an African country today the self-declared Christians
are those who raise questions about the state. If that is true, I
would like you to elaborate a bit more, because I have some
problem with that.

MR. SANNEH: I have written a paper partly in response to Geertz,
but especially in response to John Hick, who applies some of
those ideas in the theological-philosophical realm. My question
to them is, however you approach the question of religion,
somewhere along the line you have to make a transition—to my
mind an unsatisfactory transition—from the cultural representation of God to the idea of God. There is a gap there, a missing
link. I do not know what it is. You know Max Muller's famous
statement that religion is a disease of language, a disease that he
promptly tried to cure by philological means. That is rather like
the cure of the disease lying in the disease itself. If language is
the disease of religion, then why go to religion to remedy the
disease? Max Muller regretted that phrase; it followed him
through the rest of his life. Anyway, that is my problem
with Geertz and Hick as well. My reference to African political
leaders who are also Christians, who are raising fundamental
questions about the nature of political authority, really has to do
with writings and thought of people like Nyerere and Kaunda
and others. When I was in Zaire, one of the issues of the time in

the seventies was Mobutu's program of *authenticité*. Right next door in Zambia, Victor Turner was describing an investiture ritual: before a ruler was crowned he was brought out into the bush, stripped, and made to sit on a stool; people then heaped insults on the ruler, reversing the roles and reminding him that when he was fully invested he must remember not to be crooked in the administration of justice. I have always thought I must write Mobutu a letter in which I cite that and ask that it be included in the program of *authenticité*. [Laughter] But that sort of ritual example shows you in traditional Africa how people conceive of political authority. Now, this same religious principle of curtailing the power of the state and also seeing authority in terms of its efficacy—what it can *do*—is very much there in Nyerere's thought, in Kaunda's thought. It is also there in Ghanaian political nationalist writings. Christian Africa has fed into this, has developed this. My disappointment is that this has not been reflected at the academic level in African universities. Political scientists in Africa have not really drawn on this material, in the same way that African psychologists have not, to my mind, drawn on the dream materials that are there in our villages. This is the gap I feel exists between the new African elite intellectual class and the old Africa. We need to close that gap.

DATE DUE

JAN 1 8 2007			